Desertwalk

A Search for Secrets of the Desert

Written & Illustrated by Audrey Schumacher Moe

Walk Publishing

Published by
Walk Publishing, LLC
14505 Yerxa Road
Desert Hot Springs, CA 92240

Desertwalk   A Search for Secrets of the Desert
ISBN 978-0-9749885-1-1
Library of Congress Control Number 2008929182

For purchase information please contact:
desertwalk@walkpublishing.com

Printed in South Korea

Written & Illustrated by Audrey Schumacher Moe
Graphic Design by Orlando Ramos | DonGatoGraphics.com

This book is dedicated to any-one who has ever gazed in awe at a scenic vista, thrilled at the sound of a bird's distinctive call, inhaled the sweet scent of a flower in bloom, enjoyed the clean smell of the land after a rain, or taken a walk just to feel the wind blowing free. I would hope that would include everyone.

The single line
and broken fret
designs used on
the title pages
are adapted from
prehistoric Sikyatki
pueblo ware and
were used on the
exteriors of ancient
Hopi bowls.

Acknowledgments

My first book was *Beachwalk, An Everyday Journey Through Sea, Sand and Soul,* which included over 100 of my watercolor paintings along with the text. As a result of many years of work and the help of a wide variety of friends and colleagues, it gave me the experience and desire to set out on a new venture and begin the chapters and drawings for *Desertwalk, A Search for Secrets of the Desert.*

Of those who helped me along this journey, I am especially indebted to my daughter, Holly Moe, who lives on the property here at Bubbling Wells Ranch and alerted me to nature's miracles I would have missed without her reports. And to Drew Foster, the ranch foreman, who brought new wonders and natural gifts to my door and told me where to find others. Always on hand to suggest and counsel, my Wednesday afternoon critique group organized through the Palm Springs Writers Guild, listened patiently and relayed their thoughts. As we sat around the table at the Palm Desert Library and took turns presenting our work, I could count upon intelligent and worthwhile advice.

Fellow writers, Gordon Gumpertz, Gordon Davis, Mary Olson, Joanna Jacobs, Roberta Dinow, and Peg Moran encouraged me with their positive comments and appreciation of each new desert secret I uncovered in my daily ramblings through sand and sage. Roberta Dinow read the work in its entirety to catch errors or inconsistencies. Mary Shields checked grammar and spelling for which I'm very grateful. A long time friend, Marilyn Sutton, gave me sound advice on meeting the needs of my audience.

I particularly thank those faithful readers of *Beachwalk,* who kept in touch with cards and letters and periodically asked for *Desertwalk* long before it was finished. Above all, I thank my husband, Courtney, who put up with all of the time I spent writing and painting instead of being a good companion. I could not have brought out this book without his help in handling the technicalities involved in the publishing of *Desertwalk, A Search for Secrets of the Desert.*

Surprise appearance of desert mushrooms after a rain storm.

Desertwalk | VIII

Desertwalk, A Search for Secrets of the Desert came about as a direct result of a move my husband and I made from the beach to the desert. This change in our life was never planned and came about only because of a brief newspaper advertisement for a property that sounded too good to be true. We checked it out more for a lark than serious consideration and found ourselves captivated with the idea of an adventurous move that would change our lives in ways we couldn't imagine.

Leaving our much-loved home on the edge of the ocean was not an easy decision. But once made, moving to a different environment created excitement and anticipation. Learning about our new desert home and its surroundings as I climbed over wind-blown dunes and walked down sandy smoke tree-decorated washes became a daily routine that begged to be recorded as each new day offered up a different prize. I was like a child on my first trip to Disneyland, seeing and experiencing a world of wonder.

Those walks recreated on the pages of *Desertwalk* soon made it clear the desert is a place like no other and holds its secrets so tightly the casual observer may never experience their unique beauty or pathos. But as I learned how to read desert paths and gained the patience to wait for outbursts of bloom after a long-awaited rain, searched for animal life in the cool early morning hours or at twilight, the pages of *Desertwalk* began to unfold like dry leaves soaking up rain.

Whether you have looked at an expanse of desertscape and said, "There's nothing there." or whether you are a long time desert dweller, the stories in *Desertwalk* will paint a rich and varied picture of a desert you may not have known existed.

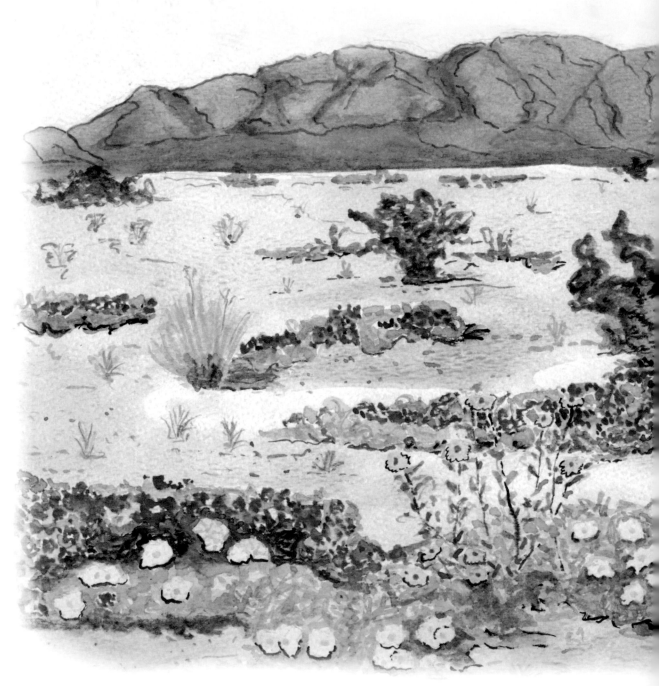

"Not everyone can tramp through desert shrub or hike sandy canyon bottoms. But almost everyone can read and vicariously experience the adventures of those who do."

Introduction

My Life began in the upstairs bedroom of a small clapboard-covered farmhouse in Wisconsin. There were already six children in the family, and four years later twins were born making the final count nine. Whether my birth was difficult or routine no one has told me, but my oldest sister once revealed that I was born with a caul (membrane) over my face. I had to look up that word and found that it's also called a holy or lucky hood. One of the superstitions attached to it is that it's a sign of good luck. Another states that if preserved, it's a protection against drowning. I have no dried up membrane tucked away in a bureau drawer, but so far I haven't drowned either. So maybe I'm just lucky. If I am to give any validity to the superstitions associated with being born with a caul, I choose luck for the fortunate combination of circumstances that brought me to the desert.

My mother was not so lucky, in that her too-short life ended at age thirty-four. Her death certificate listed cancer of the mastoids (those little bones behind the ears), but there is a good chance she really died of a massive and chronic infection. Ear aches were an affliction she endured on a regular basis and antibiotics were not yet available, so infections often became killers. There is no way I'll ever know for sure, but perhaps, due to my own bout with cancer which I talk about in an earlier book, *Beachwalk,* I think she died of an infection which, for reasons I don't understand, is more acceptable to me than cancer.

I don't remember anything from those early years on the farm. I am told by my oldest sister that at one time, in my toddler days, my mother heard my small child's voice echoing from under the front porch where I sometimes used to play in the sand after crawling through a hole in the lattice work. "Nice kitty, nice kitty," I repeated over and over. Since we didn't have any house cats, my mother asked my older sister to squeeze under the stoop and see what I was up to. There I was, sitting in the dirt cuddling a baby skunk to my cheek with the rest of the litter curled up in my lap.

I suppose any three-year-old would find a nest of black and white striped "kitties" quite appealing, but I like to think of the incident as my first wildlife encounter, one that would imprint itself upon my young brain and brand it for all time with a love for nature's wild creatures.

In reality, it was likely my brothers cultivated a good deal of my feeling for the outdoors after the family moved to another farm in northern Minnesota. Or perhaps they merely built upon what began with "kitties" under the porch. They introduced me to birds' nests in the barn eaves, pink sweet-smelling wild roses sprawling along fence lines, snapping turtles sunning on floating logs and deer wandering into the barnyard at dusk for a lick at the salt block set out for our cows. These events were always presented as something special, out of the ordinary and worthy of time spent observing and appreciating.

There were times when my brothers were just plain boys,

dancing around me, dangling a grass snake in my face while I screamed in terror, or laughing when an aggressive goose chased me with loud quacking, flapping wings and an open beak ready to pinch. Touching the electric fence with a tall stem of grass to feel the thump, thump of electricity coursing through our bodies was a game we used to see who was the bravest.

Another time, while playing around in the barn during milking hours, one of my brothers threw a pail of skim milk in my face, drenching my hair and clothes down to my shoes. I retreated to the house to change my sopping wet shorts and shirt and wash away the souring residue, but I couldn't even tell on him because I knew I had been acting really bratty and deserved what I got.

Certainly the farm environment was an important element in learning respect for nature and finding awe in its everyday events. Whether a love of nature is a trait we are born with or one developed through access and education, I do not know. I suspect there are some who, if they were raised the way I was, might want to escape to the city and never look at another bird's nest in their lifetime.

But most children, I think, are intrigued with the way plants grow and animals live. That's why grade school teachers conduct simple experiments with sprouting beans on wet paper towels and growing foliage on sweet potatoes suspended in water with toothpicks stuck in their sides to hold them in a Mason jar. Classroom teachers also keep small animals in habitats so children can observe and understand them better. I can't help but think most of us would appreciate the wild outdoor world if only we had safe and reasonable access to it.

Not everyone can tramp through desert shrub or hike sandy canyon bottoms. But almost everyone can read and vicariously experience the adventures of those who do. My current home on a large unspoiled desert property, provides the perfect acreage for me to hike safely and experience the desert.

So when I write about the Verdin's nest I watched the sparrows tear apart, two juvenile Sidewinder Rattlesnakes that took up residence in my house during remodeling, coyotes yipping their evening song, the bobcat slinking around the tractor shed at twilight, or the pottery shards and Indian metate unearthed after a rain storm, these are my offerings to those who would walk with me as well as all who cannot or would prefer not to experience such occurrences first hand.

Desertwalk, with its tales of adventures and detailed paintings, is my sweet potato in a jar growing leaves to demonstrate how nature works, my beans sprouting on wet paper towels. The property I walk daily is my terrarium where the miracles of life and death in the desert reveal their mysteries and educate me about a world I never imagined as a child growing up on a Minnesota farm.

I invite you to come with me on my desert walks to explore and observe beauty hidden in the sands of a dry and unfamiliar land. Together we will journey towards an understanding of the desert and, along the way, discover holiness inherent in all living things.

With ample fall and winter rain, Coulter's Lupine *(Lupinus sparsiflorus)* creates a vista of purple. In Texas a similar plant is called a bluebonnet.

Chapters

In wet years Desert Sand Verbena *(Abronia villosa)* carpets sandy hills and desert floor.

"Nothing can bring you peace but yourself."

–Ralph Waldo Emerson

Jackhammers and Quail

I've come out to the garden where I sit next to the pond and try to restore peace to my jangled nerves. I had to get away from the deafening racket of jackhammers ripping up a tiled pool in the entryway of my home. Since early morning, the workmen with their power tools have been busy reducing tile and concrete to piles of rubble they load into a wheelbarrow and trundle outside to a dumpster. I don't see how the jackhammer operators can stand the body-racking thrust of the machines and ever present dust. They tell me it's rewarding to work with heavy equipment and they're proud of their skills. But for me, noise is disturbing. It leaves me feeling unsettled, annoyed and short-tempered.

In the quiet of the garden I avoid most of the jarring sounds and begin to feel less tense. A quail calls from somewhere on the sloped bank above the pond. Sitting very still, so I will not alarm them, I watch as three grayish-brown birds make their way along the bank pecking at the ground. Their heads bob up and down displaying little feather top-knots that stand up like banners announcing their clan.

A soft rustle in the bushes catches my attention as two more of the pudgy birds emerge from the tall, dry grass and race across an open spot, their feather flags aiming straight ahead as if pointing the way. Four more follow. They pause in the shade of a creosote bush, but soon scatter, each searching for its own food, while continuing to stay together in a loose group.

These are Gambel's quail (*Callipepla gambelii*) named by William Gambel in the 1840's, after observing flocks of them along the Santa Fe Trail. The first half of their scientific name, *Callipepla*, comes from two Greek words meaning beautiful robe, which indeed describes the male's plumage. He is elegantly clothed with rich, gray-brown body feathers streaked with chestnut and white on his flanks, a cream-colored belly marked by a conspicuous black patch in the center, a black face rimmed with white, and a reddish-brown crown embellished by the head plume or top-knot which looks like one feather but is actually six that overlap. The female lacks the distinctive black and white face, crown and black belly patch. Her coloring is better suited than the male for birds that rely on hiding from predators, rather than flying away.

Gambel's quail spend most of their time on the ground using their strong legs as they forage for seeds, plant parts and sometimes even leaves and grass. Unlike long pointed wings of raptors, their wings are stubby and rounded, allowing them to fly, but only for short distances. When I come upon them in the wild, they scatter and run off. The only times I see them fly are when I surprise them. Then they disperse quickly, each with a loud ruffle of wing-beats.

As the most arid-adapted of any of the chicken-like birds, such as partridges, grouse, pheasants and turkeys, they are gregarious and social and mate for life although they seldom survive more than four years.

Quail hang out together in coveys. The calls I hear allow them to wander independently as they forage for food, but yet stay in the same general area as the rest of the group. Their distress or alarm cries are quite different and easy to distinguish from their normal "I'm over here" sounds made during group feeding.

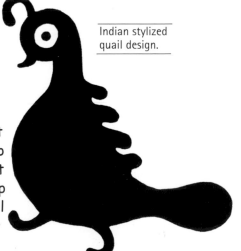

Indian stylized quail design.

A few weeks earlier as I sat reading the paper, I glanced up at just the right time to spot one of the males hop to the top of a boulder next to a small pool in the rocks above the upper pond. As I watched, another quail marched down to the pool's edge, dipped in its beak, then pointed it upward to swallow. Following quickly in single file, a line of birds reminding me of a kindergarten class, arrived to drink and scurry back into the bushes.

Finally, one of them exchanged places with the lookout on the boulder, allowing that bird its turn at the pool, then they all disappeared up the hill. During this time, not one sound betrayed them. If I had not accidentally looked up when I did, I would never have observed the system they worked out for drinking safely from a precious watering spot in the desert.

Not many days later, I discovered why they had been so quiet. That morning I looked up from my paper to see what was causing the commotion taking place at the same pond. Loud *ka, ka's* punctuated the usual morning stillness. Unable to see what was going on, I got up from my chair and quietly approached the small pool. There, almost out of sight, sat Karnac, the outside cat, poised and ready to pounce upon any unwary bird coming down to drink.

Almost the same color as the rocks, Karnac's mottled gray and hazel-colored fur blended in perfectly with the morning shadows. I never would have seen her if not for the quails' calls of alarm. Fortunately for the covey, an alert bird blew Karnac's cover so she had no quail for breakfast that day. I wouldn't even think of hunting the quail on my property, but Karnac doesn't know the rules.

When I moved to the desert I

had no idea quail were a part of desert wildlife. I should have guessed they were common, since I've seen them used as a motif on Native American pottery, both contemporary and ancient. From carved semi-precious stone Zuni fetishes to stylized versions painted on Acoma pottery, quail played a role in the lives of desert people. Hohokam pot shards dating back over 500 years depict images of quail and quail feathers. Most amazing to me are the baskets made by northern California Indians. Tiny top-knot quail plumes are spaced around the rims and woven into the basket sides. To work with something so small and delicate, and to incorporate it into a woven utensil, takes more skill than I can begin to imagine.

Quail methods of socializing and group habitation don't seem so different from some we use in our civilization. But then I think maybe it's the other way around. Perhaps at a time in the distant past, humans learned from quail that staying to-gether in a group was safer than individu-als alone. One sentinel could safeguard many and orphaned young could be raised by the community.

Painted gourd with quail design.

Keeping in constant touch vocally is a system we currently carry to an extreme by the advent of cell phones. I'm not sure this habit is one we really needed to adopt. At least we haven't picked up on the quail method of bathing, which is to wallow in the dust, although therapeutic mud baths at spas do seem related, and as a friend reminded me, in Medieval Europe, there was a practice of bathing in dust because water was "bad."

Quail babies are about as cute as anything can be. They are born precocial which means they can run and hide and feed themselves just hours after they hatch. Newly hatched ducks are also precocial (from Latin meaning "early ripening") and can swim as well as run.

The first time I saw a line of two-inch-high, newly-hatched baby quail following an adult bird across the sand, all I could think of was wind-up toys. Little beige balls of fluff toddling along, hardly big enough to climb out of a footprint in the sand, really make me marvel at how precious and precarious life can be. So small are the new hatchlings they can even be snatched away by roadrunners for a quick meal. Out of a clutch of twelve eggs, probably only three will survive to adulthood. Being cute doesn't save these babies from predators or accidents.

I'm curious about the purpose of the quail's topknot feather. It sticks up out of the head in such an abrupt manner, I can't help thinking it must have a very special purpose, like cats' whiskers that are thought to help the cat sense how wide a space it can fit through.

Courtship is the usual answer for distinct plumages, but both the male and female have the topknot and it is the male who performs the courtship ritual. Calling loudly over and over to attract a female, he stands tall to show off the black patch on his belly and sometimes entices the female with a tidbit of food. Taking ones beloved out to dinner seems to be universal.

While I would like to know more about quail, some things should just remain a mystery. I need mysteries to entice me down new paths. The anticipation of discovery is often more intriguing than the discovery itself. The great explorers of the world always had a quest, but in many cases it was the exploring itself that held the most value, rather than the journey's end.

So focused and preoccupied am I with watching the quail, I realize I have blocked out everything else around me. It is with surprise, I notice the distant jackhammer noise from the house has stopped. Intense healing silence has returned to the garden. Perhaps the men are taking a break.

The quail have wandered off and I no longer hear their calls. I don't know how they feel about noise, but I do know they inhabit remote areas, unlike pigeons that thrive in cities alongside people, buses and cars. Maybe the men working the jackhammers are like pigeons, thriving on noise and activity. I know for certain that I am like the quail, needing space and serene quiet surroundings.

Gambel's quail eggs found in abandoned nest on ground under a palm leaf.

"The miracles of nature do not seem miracles because they are so common."

–Anonymous

A New World

When I moved to the Coachella Valley of Southern California, I was not so naive as to expect only endless sand dunes and rattlesnakes, but I really knew very little about true desert life. I was aware the weather was warm, sometimes very warm, but I had no idea what it would be like to spend a summer with the mercury climbing upwards past 110 degrees. And I had no idea that cold winter nights could occasionally dip below freezing.

The draw of my new home was a large unimproved acreage, the luxury of our own wells for irrigation water, and wild, raw native desert surrounding us like a medieval moat. The opportunity to explore and experience this land, untouched as yet by new housing and paved streets, drew me like a magnet to metal.

In the past, my mental picture of a desert was a panorama of cactus and sand, a barren vista with miles of emptiness dominated by relentless sun. I knew there was more than that in the Coachella Valley. I had already spent a little time in Palm Springs, perhaps the city best known world wide, of the nine or so occupying the basin between the Santa Rosa and Little San Bernardino mountain chains.

I had already experienced the irrigated desert with palm trees swaying gently in the breeze, air-conditioned houses nestled in yards with swimming pools, green grass and flowers. All made possible with water pumped from a huge underground aquifer. But this was not the desert I had come to explore.

As attuned as I was to the many moods of the beach, a home I had just left, learning the rhythms and cycles of a new landscape was a choice my husband and I had made and I was eager to begin the adventure.

Desert – the word alone can strike fear into the hearts of many who envision a barren land with endless miles of blowing sand and scorching heat. Yet, desert is merely the name of a landform like mountain, coastal plain, beach, etc. Any terrain with ten inches or less of rainfall per year is defined as desert and about one-third of the planet's landmass falls into this category. Almost all of the

"In the past, my mental picture of a desert was a panorama of cactus and sand, a barren vista with miles of emptiness dominated by relentless sun."

Agave – a wide variety of agaves thrive in the desert

major deserts exist within a belt around the planet extending thirty degrees north and thirty degrees south of the equator.

Weather patterns create different kinds of deserts. The Coachella Valley of Southern California is a "rain shadow" desert. The mountains to the west literally shield the valley from rain. As moist air blowing east from the western Pacific coast rises to pass over the San Jacinto Mountains, it drops its water on the western slopes, leaving only dry air to descend down the eastern side into the Coachella Valley.

But unlike some deserts where rain never falls or deserts which are chillingly cold, the Colorado – Sonoran Desert receives just enough rainfall *(five inches per year on average)* to support a wide variety of plants and wildlife.

In my first month of desert living, as I am feeling self-satisfied and a little smug for gleaning the definition of desert and the term "rain shadow" from my research, I am awakened one night with the sound of heavy rain thundering on the roof. All five inches of our yearly rainfall must be coming down right now, I think as I lie in bed and wonder if there will be water damage to repair the next day.

When I get up and go for a walk the next morning, I am shocked to see how the downpour has changed the landscape. Our gravel road is covered with several inches of fine silt where a wide flow of water followed a shallow wash, fanned out across the road and dug a two-foot deep channel as it continued on over the lower third of our property. Uprooted desert bushes are piled high against a chain link fence where the flood passed through on its way downhill. Other areas where the water rushed through are scoured clean.

This is my first lesson in desert landscaping. A land of sparse water is nevertheless dominated and formed by water. Flash floods create washes and arroyos, carve out canyons, sculpt mountain crags, and carry sand down from high peaks to form alluvial fans.

As winter softens and the days begin to warm, spring winds rear their gritty heads and I am faced with another powerful desert force. Rapidly rising and falling air, brought about by seasonal temperature changes, creates winds that course across the sands, scouring the ground, building dunes of loose granules, and polishing rocks with blowing grit.

So it doesn't take long for me to discover the desert is ruled by water, wind and extremes of temperature. A much longer learning curve, I find, is necessary for acquiring a knowledge of resident plants and animals.

My new home located where the northern edge of the Sonoran Desert abuts the southern tip of the Mojave has a climate with elements of both high and low deserts, so I can count on an even richer environment than either desert alone. Crossover flora and fauna from both deserts can thrive in this zone 900 to 1,000 feet above sea level. Learning how adaptations to the climate allow survival in this sometimes harsh environment is my next assignment.

I buy several books on cactus or cacti, I don't yet know which is the correct plural, and excitedly pour over them in the evening to become acquainted with the multitude of different varieties. Soon I discover there are only a few types growing wild that I will encounter on my walks. All other bushes, trees and perennials are new to me and must be researched.

Animal life intrigues me even more, and I eagerly look for information on each new creature that crosses my path. Many of my most rewarding experiences are with casual glimpses of desert wild life appearing when I least expect it, like the bobcat crossing my path in a flash of spotted fur or the ephemeral wild flower springing out of bare ground after a rain. And, I might add, I have also not yet encountered a rattlesnake while out exploring the land. The snakes themselves, like so much of the desert, remain secretive and elusive.

My appreciation for this stark and beautiful terrain grows daily as I think of how different it is from woodlands and farmlands where I grew up, and from the California coast where I lived most of my adult years. I have experienced three distinctly different environments in my lifetime, and each one held amazing gifts of nature.

As I consider the unique aspects of differing landforms, I can't help but compare them with how people differ from one another. Some of us thrive on dry desert heat and sunshine, others are comfortable in high humidity and overcast skies. Some live where the first snowfall is a joyous event and summer a scant three months long. Yet, like the desert fringe-toed lizard that has learned to "swim" through sand, much like a fish swimming through water, each of us adapts to the circumstances of our specific environment.

Finding the pleasures inherent in our own place is a good way to live. I have a fascinating journey ahead of me as I search for secrets of the desert. Each one, I know, will surprise me in a way I could never anticipate. That is the power of nature.

Birdcage Evening Primrose – the dried stems of this plant bend outward and come together at the top, resembling a small birdcage.

"Everything has its own perfection, be it higher or lower in the scale of things..."

-John Henry Newman

Creepy Critters

With sun filtering through leafy branches of a grapefruit tree, I sit at the round wooden patio table, the newspaper spread out before me, as I eat my morning cereal. A small rustling sound catches my attention and I look up just in time to see a cocky roadrunner spear a bug from its hiding place in some dry leaves caught between two rocks. "Good morning, Mrs. Roadrunner," I say out loud. "Nice of you to join me for breakfast." The bird looks at me, tilts its head sideways and struts a few steps closer.

I'm not the only one having breakfast outside, I think.

One of the things I love most about the desert is living outdoors almost as much as indoors. I can enjoy the wildlife around my home, mosquitoes are almost non-existent because of the dry climate, and pesky houseflies are seldom seen except for a brief period in the spring. Outdoor living is the norm in this land of year round warm temperatures, clear blue skies and sunny days.

The desert lacks annoying swarms of outside insects that plague high humidity climates. But even here insects thrive, they just have different environmental habits.

My first encounter with big bugs took place in the library and TV room with the appearance of inch-long cockroaches. Usually they were dead, flopped over on their backs with spindly legs sticking straight up in the air. Other

Common desert centipede, uses poison from front fangs to subdue small prey. Bite may be painful to humans, but harmless.

times, when I tried to sweep one into a dustpan, it quickly scurried away into a crack in the woodwork.

Next they showed up in the pantry and utility room. They were by far the biggest cockroaches I have ever seen. *As long as I don't see them in the bedroom,* I thought, *I can handle it.*

But I soon found out the bedroom was not off limits to small creepy critters. Terrified squealing one morning from the two women who help me clean my house brought me running from the kitchen. They had uncovered a three-inch-long centipede hiding under the shower mat. The cleaners are repulsed by insects and, consequently, seem destined to run into them more often than I do. As usual, they sought me out to rescue them from this disgusting intruder.

My system for taking care of unwanted outside bugs that have taken up residence indoors is to grab a plastic drinking cup and ease the critter into it with a scrap of stiff paper as a pusher, then set the cup upright with the trapped insect inside. This works for almost anything except crickets. A cricket will leap out unless I have a cover, but since they don't bite, I can use my free hand to keep it trapped while I carry the cup outside to release the cricket into its natural environment.

The three-inch centipede the cleaners expected me to rescue them from was a bug I had never before seen in the house. I was curious to know something about this rather large multi-legged specimen so, instead of releasing it, I set it aside in its plastic cup until I could look it up in one of my books on insects.

Several days went by before I remembered the bug in the cup and, when I finally checked on it, the imprisoned centipede appeared lifeless and I felt guilty for killing it through my negligence. I jiggled the container just to be sure and the centipede came quickly to life.

"Giant desert hairy scorpion, one of nature's oldest creatures remaining unchanged for 450 million years stings with its tail. It can exist without food for a year."

With camera ready, I dumped the centipede onto a sheet of paper where its darker body would show up against the white background. Hoping it wouldn't scamper away, I was poised, cup in hand, ready to recapture it if necessary. Instead, it coiled into a circle, a defensive position, letting me know it was alive and ready to fight back. I took the hint and, after a few close-up pictures, released it under a purple verbena plant in the front garden.

It crawled away as I watched and I thought, *There goes another morsel for the roadrunners.* Or maybe this one will escape long enough to reproduce and create more of its kind to add to the balance of nature. I'm all for letting that balance play out as long as it is not in my house.

Later, from its photograph, I was able to identify the brownish-tan centipede as a *Scolopendra polymorpha,* or common desert centipede so I may be seeing more of these. However, I'm not sure I want to run into the six to eight-inch orange and black colored giant desert centipede (*Scolopendra heros)* also described in the book.

Centipedes are found worldwide and have a painful, but non-dangerous bite. In reality, the "bite" is venom injected from pincer-like appendages in front of the legs. Desert centipedes are limited to nocturnal activities since they lack the waxy layer in their cuticle, that other arthropods have to keep them from drying up in the sun.

Just as I was thinking of centipedes as unattractive lowly creatures, I discover in my research that centipede mothers care for their eggs, coiling around them and grooming them until they hatch, then tending the young until they crawl away. So however I may react to them, I have to give them some credit for being good mothers.

The huge four inch-long scorpion the cleaners found in our bedroom several months later wasn't an especially welcome guest either. Once discovered under the edge of the dog bed in front of the fireplace, it took a defensive position, tail aimed upward ready to sting. Scooping it into the cup was easy and gave me real hero status, since both cleaning ladies were horrified at the sight of the fat, white, menacing-looking creature.

Other scorpions I have seen outside, while raking leaves or moving stones in the garden, have been much smaller than this one hiding in the house. I tried not to think about the possibility of accidentally stepping on it at night in the dark with my bare feet.

The first scorpion I discovered in the garden was colored a subtle, almost iridescent, pale green. Its inner organs showed through the nearly transparent body. At first glance, I actually thought it was one of those glow-in-the-dark plastic toy replicas you buy in nature museum gift shops. I quickly changed my mind when it coiled its tail upward and aimed it at me.

Of the ten species of scorpions living in the Coachella Valley, none are dangerous, although their sting can really hurt. Unlike in Mexico where several hundred people die each year from the sting of a bark scorpion, the United States hasn't had a death in fifty years. However, bark scorpions recently discovered in Arizona may be advancing into California, so staying away from scorpions is a good idea. Even so, I don't kill them.

Ever since I observed a roadrunner grab a fat one and run off to gobble it down with gusto, I know they have an important place in the food chain. Who am I to deprive the roadrunners of an occasional feast? So the scorpion found in our house was released into the garden where it belonged.

Not all societies think of scorpions as undesirable. Scorpion images are part of Native American lore, and in Thailand they are deep-fried and eaten as a snack. Jerry Hopkins, author of *Extreme Cuisine,* says they taste a lot like french-fries because "mainly what you taste is the oil and the salt." In

China, fried scorpions and fried locust larvae are offered as food sources and one travel editor reports they have a crunchy nutty flavor.

If you're not into eating scorpions, perhaps a medicinal cure is more your style. A young woman from Mexico told me how to cure arthritis with the use of a scorpion. She did a lot of laundry by hand and was having so much pain in her fingers and wrist she was miserable, until an elder gave her a recipe for a cure. Find a scorpion, put it in a bottle with alcohol, wait a few days, then rub the alcohol on your hands. She told me she knows it works because she's never had any pain since. I'm not validating this as a remedy for arthritis or suggesting anyone else try it, but, hey, it worked for her.

In the house we continue to battle giant cockroaches. I have been brought up to believe they are the result of filth, but my house is clean, so I don't know what the cockroaches are doing in it. They don't bite and are harmless, other than possibly contaminating food.

Cockroaches aren't even desert adapted and exist in our homes only because of the irrigation of our landscaped yards. They can be eliminated by pest control people who will spray your house and yard with a pesticide. I really don't like having this done because killing the insects is killing and poisoning the food for birds. I prefer to attract birds, not drive them away.

The American cockroach *(Periplaneta americana)* is often referred to in the desert as a date or palm beetle, a euphemism, I think, because "beetle" doesn't sound as disgusting as "cockroach."

My cleaners are squeamish about dead cockroaches as well as any of the live bugs, but they have finally learned to sweep a dead one onto a dustpan and carry it outside where it becomes roadrunner food. Sure, the bugs could just be put into the garbage can with other household trash, but why not feed the birds when it is so easy and takes so little effort?

It's the little things, I think, that reveal the true self, that define who we are. Small actions, a look of compassion or a smile for no obvious reason, reflect the feelings inside. Taking the time to help a neighbor or a stranger, or rescuing a small animal or bird in trouble often does more for the helper than the helpee.

Little things, like attitudes towards others, small kindnesses, offers of help and cooperation, I think of as insights into the soul of an individual. I understand that people often rise above their pettiness in times of disaster and sometimes sacrifice themselves to save others, but it's still the little things that are important on a daily basis.

Returning bugs caught in the house to their outdoor environment may seem like a silly little thing, but it helps me feel compassion for all wild creatures that must fend for themselves. Whether we like them or not, insects have been around for millions of years. Their first recorded presence in fossils comes from the murky depths of the Silurian Period, more than 400 million years ago, when plants were just developing on land and 170 million years before dinosaurs appeared. Insects have held a distinct place in the scheme of things ever since.

Feeling compassion for these little creatures helps me more than it does them, as I try to build the best life I can through one little thing after another, even when its only a bug returned to its outdoor environment.

Nests of mud dauber wasps are built in protected places and used to store paralyzed spiders for feeding of young.

"The age of discovery on this planet may be over.
But for the average person, it has hardly begun."

-Lars-Eric Lindblad

Fool's Gold

This morning's walk takes me down a recently-carved wash to where it ends in a shallow basin. Last week after a heavy winter downpour, water collected here. Now it has evaporated and all that remains is a tongue of newly deposited flood sand that fans out and terminates in a series of u-shaped raised rills. Finer-grained black silt interlaced with flecks shimmering like metallic gold, outlines each horseshoe-shaped depression. The angle of the early morning sun reflects off the fine, sparkling flakes and creates a natural bejeweled breastplate fashioned of black and gold-colored silt.

This glittering earthen necklace makes me think of when our children were young and we took family hikes. Frequently, one of us would spot gold-colored sediment lying on a stream bottom and we'd wonder if it could be gold dust. After gathering the material in our hands and looking at it in a different light, the stream treasure always turned out to be flecks of mica, called fool's gold because of its metallic luster. While we never found any real gold, the fun came from thinking it was possible.

So this morning, always on the alert for a new challenge, I gather a small amount of the speckled black silt to take home and test for the possibility it might be a deposit of gold dust. I think it will be fun to put it in a metal pie tin with water and swirl it around like the old prospectors did when they panned for the precious metal. If the yellow, metallic specks sink to the bottom they could be gold dust, since gold is heavier than silt in suspension and will remain in the pan when the water and silt are poured out.

In my mind, I don't expect it to be the real thing, even though it shines so brightly in the sun. The color is a little too brassy to be the yellow-gold found in our western states.

It was gold that pulled fortune-seekers westward and lured many to their deaths in the desert while searching for the elusive treasure. California is famous for its stories of gold strikes and the occasional lucky hiker finding a good sized nugget in a stream bed.

Those prospectors who found deposits of gold were tightlipped and secretive about their locations, and frequently couldn't rediscover the mines once they left them to replenish their food supplies or sell the ore they had accumulated.

Adding to the difficulty of identifying gold is that it occurs in many forms, some difficult to recognize. It takes a sophisticated miner to recognize black gold. When gold nuggets are covered with a film of manganese oxide, they look like hematite and never would be recognized by the neophyte gold seeker.

Of the many stories woven around black gold, one involves a small black mountain near Twentynine Palms in the Mojave Desert. This eroded volcanic chimney located in a dry lake was thought to be the source for black gold nuggets covered with manganese. The legendary Pegleg Smith was one of those who heard about the deposit and went in search of it.

Pegleg, a hardy trapper, transported furs during the early 1800's. When an Indian arrow shattered his leg bone just above the ankle, he borrowed a butcher knife and amputated his own foot. A Snake Indian woman nursed him back to health and Pegleg fashioned a wooden stump from an ash tree branch.

Black-tailed jackrabbit
(Lepus californicus)

Pegleg knew about black gold since he had picked up black pebbles that later turned out to be gold on one of his fur trading trips in 1829. Three black buttes in the rough and mountainous Colorado Desert between the Colorado River and Salton Sink marked the secret spot, but Pegleg never found his way back to what became known as The "Lost Valley of the Phantom Buttes." Many others have since tried unsuccessfully to find it, but it remains a mystery.

In his search for gold, Pegleg heard about another source of black gold. A volcanic chimney in the Mojave Desert near Joshua Tree Nation Park and the town of Twentynine Palms was supposedly littered with the precious pebbles. Whether Pegleg discovered the rich cache or not is unknown.

When he was found unconscious, suffering from hunger and thirst in the desert, he had one large black nugget in his possession. Several days later he died without regaining consciousness and left behind a continuing mystery. Did the black gold nugget come from the volcanic site or could he have taken it from the dead body of another unlucky prospector?

So many stories of gold exist in the desert; myth and fact, colored by exaggeration and tall tales to entertain, blur together to comprise the rich and colorful lore of early desert life. On principle alone, I am compelled to check out the glitter in the wash I came upon this morning.

The only container I can find for collecting a sample is a Kleenex I carefully fold to create a kind of envelope. Even so, a portion of the fine dust leaks out and settles in the bottom of my pocket.

At home, after my walk, I empty the wrapped sample and pour its contents into a metal pie tin, add water and swirl it around to see if any of the glitter will sink as the water and silt wash over the edge of the pan. Just as I had thought before I began, the sparkling material is mica. My pan holds only a romantic idea of what might have been.

Black Phoebe

How often, I think, do we search for the elusive gold in our lives and end up, instead, with only a glittery imitation. As I get older, it seems easier to avoid the newest fad, the "must have" item advertised heavily, the newest computer program, gadget, current movie or latest fashion. Not that these can't be fun or useful, but so often they end up as momentary glitter, like fool's gold with no intrinsic worth.

And sometimes, the most important or lasting qualities are like black gold, covered with a layer of commonplace, a disguise that conceals the treasure within. I search for gold daily, not the shiny yellow metal, but lasting values and ways of living that define a life and make it the best it can be under the circumstances surrounding it.

On the same walk where I collected the fool's gold, I watched a cottontail sitting motionless until I came too close and caused it to rush away in panic. I stopped and listened while a male Gambel's quail atop a fencepost called its covey together. A lone blacktailed jackrabbit with ears like pink sentinel flags bounded through the desert brush as I approached, and small delicate desert doves rested in the shade under the low boughs of a creosote bush. Even the tiny gray-brown birds that flitted in and around as they searched for insects in the twiggy branches of an Indigo plant were a pleasure to watch.

Young cottontail

"These were the gold of my morning walk. The fool's gold merely served to remind me the true gold of life is sometimes disguised, but it is there awaiting any prospector willing to look for it."

"... every walk is a sort of crusade..."

-Henry David Thoreau

Alone in the Desert

In cool morning air of a desert winter, I hike rapidly down a sandy wash near my home with only my dog for company. Now is the time to go as far as we can before the heat of day sets in. Geronimo is a good companion. He doesn't talk, he follows where I go and lends a bit of safety to my walks around the ranch. We enjoy the desert together, he relying on his superb sense of smell, while I depend upon visual stimulation to bring me pleasure.

I choose to walk without human companions because I need to experience the desert without distraction, unencumbered and freed from the daily trivia of living. I walk to soak up the spirit of the place, to feel the peace, the quiet, and the enrichment gained from solitude. Even casual conversation would take my thoughts away from this land born of eroded rock and windswept vistas. Alone and on my own is the best way for me to reach into my soul and reveal myself through nature.

My friends sometimes caution me about going by myself. I understand their concern, but my walks with Geronimo are perfectly safe. All of them are within the hundred acres surrounding my home. I cannot get lost and I carry a cell phone for any emergency.

For long hikes in remote areas unfamiliar to me, I wouldn't dream of going alone and would follow good, sensible hiking rules. Group hiking and walking alone are two entirely different things with different goals and different rewards.

A group hike my husband and I went on in the Florida Everglades would not have been possible to take alone, but in the company of others, and two knowledgeable leaders, it became a memorable highlight of the canoe trip we were on one January.

It was midmorning when our group of fifteen in street clothes and tennis shoes lined up to follow our leader through chest-deep, black, ominous-looking water. Over-hanging tree limbs strung with swags of blue-green moss blocked out most of the sun, leaving only a pale, eerie half-light. Spiky-leaved epiphites clung to branches and trunks of woody shrubs rooted in swamp mud.

It was the same place where, the night before, we had followed a wooden walkway with flashlights in hand but deliberately turned off. Beneath overgrown trees festooned with hanging Spanish moss, and air as quiet and thick as oil, we felt our way along the planks, and at a whispered signal from our guide, turned on our lights and aimed them into the swamp. Everywhere, it seemed, pairs of small red-reflecting eyes dotted the black water. Alligators - all around us. But we were safe on the wood plank walkway above the reach of vicious jaws.

The next morning, ready to walk unprotected into that same inky water inhabited by the alligators we'd seen the night before, I couldn't imagine how we could do this until our guide explained that by walking in a line, we ceased to be prey for the 'gators and became, instead, one huge critter with multiple legs. All of us together merged into a gigantic beast, far too large for any alligator to even think about attacking. Together we were a threat, and any 'gators in the area would slink away to hide from us. I believed the guide or I never could have placed so much as a toe into that alligator-infested swamp.

As we slogged along, one behind the other like dominoes, chest deep in brackish water the color of black coffee, I couldn't see my hand under the surface, much less my feet. I never knew what I was stepping on, perhaps a sunken tree trunk, nest of water-logged branches that caught at my ankles, or sometimes a soft squishy unknown object I didn't dare think about. In the almost opaque water, all I could do was follow the person ahead of me as closely as possible and hope I didn't trip and fall.

After a short time, the walk didn't seem quite so intimidating except for my concern about snakes. I knew the swamp was the home of cottonmouth water moccasins and other kinds of snakes, not all of which are venomous. But I really didn't want to see any kind of snake swimming next to me. An even greater fear was that a snake might drop onto me from the trees above my head. Our leader assured us any snake in the water would slither off just like the 'gators and he would shoo away any reptiles hanging from the trees before we got to them.

Obviously, this walk through a portion of the Florida Everglades could only take place in a group. With lots of kidding and comments on the intimidating and scary trek we were sharing, that hour spent shuffling along in alligator and snake-infested water turned out to be a highlight of the trip, because it was so far from anything I would ever undertake by myself.

Group forays into the wild have their value and introduce us to adventures we could never experience on our own. There is no doubt the group hike in the Everglades revealed a truth for me.

Desert Marigold-
Marigold comes from
"Mary's Gold," a
reference to Virgin Mary.

I proved to myself I was brave enough to wade through the black water home of alligators and snakes. But it required the support of fourteen other people and two guides to make it safe. Having done it, I feel empowered by the knowledge I could participate in an activity stretching the limits for me.

Enjoying nature is why I walk alone in the wash this morning. Today as I follow the serpentine course carved out by water, I feel a sense of peace. With eons of time to make its mark, water seeks its own level and the path of least resistance. I, too, am learning to flow gently, to enjoy being wherever I am, knowing the next step and next moment will come soon enough.

Being alone is different from being lonely. By myself, my senses come alive. The warmth of the sun infuses my body with power. The touch of a breeze on my skin is like a lover's caress. The landscape cradles me with security and a feeling of well-being. I become a part of the earth, belonging to it and growing out of it like plants pulling their nourishment from the soil. Surely the great naturalists like John Muir, Thoreau, and Emerson, who translated his feelings into poetry, experienced all of these emotions as they explored and lived alone in the outdoors.

When my mind is open and I am quiet, the sensory side of my environment emerges. That is when I smell wisps of herbal fragrance, savor the caress of a warm breeze, follow the trail of a tiny beetle crossing my path, or stop and feel the texture of yellow petals on a Desert Marigold. Any tensions I may have fly away in the breeze and I feel unburdened. These are sensations difficult to share with others. They are as intimate as one's deepest thoughts and worst fears.

As I stroll through the desert alone, I am never lonely. The walk itself, is poetry in three dimensions. It sings and rhymes and composes pictures. Sand sparkling in the sunlight becomes the fairy dust of imagination left over from one stroke of Mother Nature's magic wand as she transforms the land through the seasons.

"Just as a dry stick studded with thorns pushes out green leaves after a rain, my stimulated mind grows new ideas. I become a part of nature instead of apart from nature. I am brought to the realization that my one true place on earth is anywhere I can see and feel the elements that nourish all living things."

Safe Hiking rules

- Don't go hiking by yourself, take along a friend.
- Tell someone else where you are going and don't change your route.
- Let others know when you expect to return.
- Pay attention to the weather and prepare for it.
- Take more water than you think you will need.

"The most beautiful and most profound emotion
we experience is the sensation of the mystical."

- Dr. Albert Einstein

Something Special

On a winter morning, while taking a walk before sunrise, the sky hangs above me like a blanket of black velvet. I reach upward wishing I could feel the darkness with my finger tips, stroke its texture with my hand. But dawn, ready to display its shining rays, takes over gently and black begins its shift to darkest blue. Then, like water added to paint, it thins to an icy cerulean studded with gray.

I follow a loop trail along the ridge line of a hill and shiver in the cool, humid air. A residue of moisture left over from recent heavy rains obscures the glow of the rising sun, and layers of dense clouds to the east screen out the usual morning sky colors of mauve and gold that precede daylight in the desert.

A faint rustling in dry leaf debris under bushes betrays efforts of small nocturnal creatures as they search for shelter and safety from exposure to daylight and discovery by predators. I listen to short staccato chirps coming from somewhere in the branches of a mesquite tree and stop to enjoy the plaintive *coo-coo* of a mourning dove signaling the beginning of a new day. On top of the hill, the distant hum of traffic on the interstate over five miles away carries across the desert scrub and reminds me of the busy world outside of the ranch borders.

Returning home I go about my duties of the day. I feed both cats, Betty inside in the laundry room and Karnak outside on top of a cabinet. Betty hangs around me and gets under my feet from the moment I get out of bed, but I have to call for Karnak, who is already skulking around the garden looking for a moving target to pounce upon.

I toss fish food to the pond koi who hang out near a cluster of partially-submerged boulders. They swim frantically about while greedily gulping the small pellets. A few smaller fish, added within the last few months, hide under the remains of water lilies past their prime summer bloom. In time, I expect they, too, will react enthusiastically to their morning feeding.

I am looking forward to my own breakfast and coffee when one of the ranch hands arrives with something to show me.

He carries a towel-covered bundle measuring about twelve by eighteen inches across the top and four to five inches thick. I assume it must be a flat box with something in it. I'm thinking possibly a snake or a lizard. Or maybe, because he holds it as if it's very heavy, it contains the big tortoise we've seen several times down near the plant nursery.

He sets it on a sturdy bench, whips off the towel with a magician's flourish and says, "How about that?" I can hardly believe my eyes. It's a stone *metate*.

This flat rectangle of rock has been beautifully hand-shaped with rounded corners, its worn, slightly depressed center the result from countless hours of grinding hard seeds. I touch it and let my fingers flow over its smooth satiny rock face. There is no doubt this is the real thing, a grinding stone from the past.

Stone *metate* used for pulverizing seeds, found in desert wash – 12x18 inches

"Where did you get this?" I ask. The ranch hand tells me how he was over on the northeast corner of the property in Hildalgo Wash clearing some brush out of a channel cut by recent rains.

"I noticed the rounded edge of a rock sticking out of a new bank created by run-off water," he says. "Only a small curved portion showed and I felt drawn to it, but nothing about it indicated it was more than a common boulder, so I ignored it and went on with my work.

The next day I couldn't get the stone out of my mind. I was so drawn to it that I went back to the site to satisfy my curiosity. When I dug the rock out of the sandy bank, I knew it was something special.

I felt a mysticism, a spiritual power coming from it, he said. "It was so strong, it pulled me back even after I had left it in place when I first saw it. It was the same color as other rocks in the area, there wasn't anything different about it that showed, but I just felt it was something I had to go to.

I hope you don't mind," he continued, "but I took it home with me over the weekend. I wanted it in my house for a while because I felt it was so powerful. I knew I could bring it back to you on Monday."

Needless to say, I am thrilled with the artifact, and since it affected another person so deeply, it is even more remarkable than if I had been the one to find it. I easily identify with the finder's excitement of discovery. That same type of thing has happened to me, and I understand that indescribable sense of connection with the newly-unearthed object.

Once, when walking in an arroyo with family and friends, I lagged behind, and as I ambled along I noticed a tiny bluish-tinted stone in the path where those ahead had already walked. When I kicked it out of the sand with my shoe and examined it, I found myself holding a perfectly crafted arrowhead. With sand and dirt wiped away, it was a beautiful piece of blue-white chert. Everyone else had walked over it without noticing or sensing it was there.

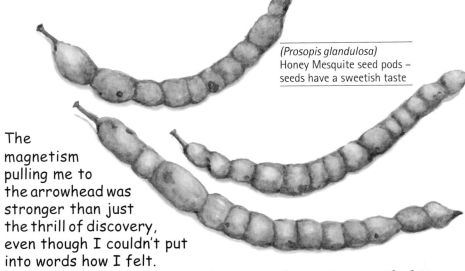

(Prosopis glandulosa)
Honey Mesquite seed pods – seeds have a sweetish taste

Both sides of a worked point

The magnetism pulling me to the arrowhead was stronger than just the thrill of discovery, even though I couldn't put into words how I felt.

An incident of this type has special meaning, as if, for some unknown reason, the object was waiting for me. I know I may be making too much of a casual coincidence, but I find life is more fun, richer and more intense when I let my feelings cast their spell during these extraordinary moments.

Now, with the newly found *metate* resting on my patio, I want to know more about how this artifact was used. Many hands over many hours pushed a smaller rounded rock, a *mano*, over this granite stone in the process of pulverizing seeds from desert plants.

Mesquite beans, one of the nutritious foods early people consumed, were likely processed on this *metate*. A friend of mine still collects the seed pods, but she grinds them in her electric mixer. She tried to convince me to try using them to make my own mesquite flour, but the beans are hard and tough, and, since I don't really enjoy cooking as a hobby, I haven't found time to fuss with them. I would like to taste pancakes made from mesquite flour, but since I can't buy it in a store, I'm going to have to wait until I become ambitious enough to make my own.

The meal made from these seeds must have taken a huge amount of time and strength when being mashed by hand with a *mano* in a stone mortar or *metate*. The *mano*, a small hand-held stone, is pushed back and forth on top of the *metate,* with the processed material crushed in between. In time the *mano* becomes smooth and rounded as any roughness wears away.

One might think it would be hard to find edible, wild food in the desert. But people found a way to use almost any plant available and the list of nutritious or at least usable desert plants is long. Jojoba beans were made into a powder to make a coffee-like drink, dried gourd seeds ground and mixed with water formed an edible mush, and even the dried fruit of California fan palms could be made into flour. Crushed ocotillo seeds with a protein content of twenty-nine percent were especially nutritious. Where saguaro and organ pipe cactus grow, a gruel for bread can be made from their seeds.

The cakes Indians formed by mixing mesquite meal with water were an ideal food for carrying on hunting or migration trips. Desert plants with nutritious, or at the least edible, seeds include many more species and most were processed by hand with a *mano* and *metate,* essential utensils for desert people.

The newly unearthed *metate,* which peeked out of the earth after the rains, is now a resident of my patio. While it is very heavy, it could have been transported short distances when a camp was moved to a more desirable area not too far away. In contrast, bedrock mortars, grinding holes in huge rock outcroppings, were stationary and could only be used seasonally as a group moved from winter to summer camps.

So this utensil was important to a family, yet it was abandoned or lost at some time in the distant past. It makes me wonder about the woman who ground her family's food on this stone. Where did she and her people come from, where did they go?

While they were here, they would have enjoyed some of the same desert sights I do. They would have observed pink and gold morning sunrises, ruby red sunsets and watched a comet streak through an inky black sky. They had to have felt warm sun on their backs and shivered in the winter rains.

I run my fingers over the *metate's* surface and follow the faint striations forced into the stone through daily usage. I think, while I can't touch the heavens of early morning, I can place my hand on a remnant of a past civilization, and in so doing I imagine the power of the object.

An essential for life, surely this stone represents a whole society. I can never really know that world, just as I can't imagine the depths of the darkest celestial space before dawn.

What I do know is that by being aware of what once was, I am better able to understand the past, and that helps me appreciate the present, whether it is a predawn black velvet sky or an ancient utilitarian artifact.

Type of *metate* and *mano* – granite, 22x12 inches

Metate with raised sides and *mano* – granite, 15x16 inches

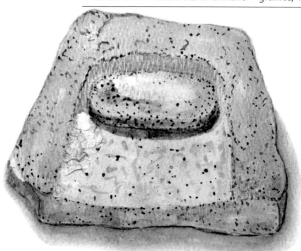

"Any glimpse into the life of an animal quickens our own and makes it so much the larger and better in every way."

- John Muir

Innocent Predator

After a brisk walk on a morning filled with the promise of spring, I decide to catch up on some of my ever-present yard work. With clippers in hand, I study the overgrown honeysuckle vine twined around one of the *portal* posts. For Santa Fe style houses, *portal* is the word used for a covered outdoor area that generally extends the length of the house. Early desert houses needed *portals* for shade from the unrelenting sun. The patio's of today's homes serve the same purpose.

I try to be careful with my trimming so I won't disturb the dove's nest buried in the dense tangled foliage. I love how the dove sits on her nest and doesn't move no matter how close I get. Sometimes her small black bead eye will follow me as I move around the plant, but if I didn't know where to look I'd never notice. I've heard people say, "Dumb doves, they sit there and don't move." But sitting motionless is a very effective camouflage technique.

One dove built a nest in plain sight on a palm frond only eighteen inches from the ground. I must have walked past it three or four times a day for a week or more before I noticed the motionless gray bird nestled into her structure of loosely intertwined twigs. Even Geronimo, the dog, did not detect the presence of the nest in spite of the fact it was exactly level with his nose.

Remaining frozen in stillness is a common way for animals in the wild to protect themselves, since stationary objects blend into the landscape. In locating prey, predator's eyes search for movement. Thousands of years ago, at a time when hunting for food was necessary for man's survival, detecting movement was a crucial ability. Today our eyes retain that same characteristic.

I climb halfway up on my stepladder to reach the highest growth as I begin clipping and coaxing sweet-smelling honeysuckle tendrils into a more aesthetic form. Sounds of a fracas taking place over near the spa catch my attention. From a corner of my eye, as I peer through a jungle of leaves and vines, I see Karnac, the outside cat, racing across the lawn, obviously after something. I drop my pruning shears, jump down off the ladder and run after the cat just in time to see her heading proudly towards the house carrying a baby bunny in her jaws.

I hurry after her, calling her name to get her attention and hopefully to slow her pace. She pauses slightly, which is just enough for me to gently grab her around her sleek, slender middle. As I pick her up, she drops

Karnac, the predator

the bunny. I hustle her inside the house, out of the way, while petting her and crooning soothingly, "Nice kitty, nice kitty, I know you can't help chasing baby bunnies. They are such easy prey. Nice kitty." I hopes she understands I am not punishing her for something instinctive in her nature.

Back outside, the bunny is desperately trying to escape to a safe place by dragging its frail little body along with its front paws, its limp, immobile hind legs leaving parallel tracks in the sand. I grab a heavy garden glove, thinking I will use it to pick up the little creature and carry it to a safe spot in the bushes to rest and maybe recover. But its wild survival instincts are set on full power and with the use of only its front legs, the bunny propels its broken body over the yard so fast I can't catch it. When it reaches a small dirt niche on the edge of the rock garden, it snuggles up to the rocks and lies there, its heart pounding so hard I can see its body pulse with each rapid beat.

My heart aches for the little creature in its frantic effort to live. I move away to avoid stressing it even more and go into the house to make sure the dog is inside and won't present the little animal with another danger.

A bit later I come out to check on the bunny. It's dead. A wave of relief along with sweet sadness sweeps over me. I knew it was severely injured and unlikely to survive in the wild, but I was not yet prepared to kill it in order to prevent further suffering. I no longer had to make the decision, the right thing had happened. I wondered if it had died from its injuries or from extreme stress. I've read that rabbits in particular can die from fright. Their heart just stops.

I remember an incident on our African trip a number of years ago. We were with a guide out viewing wildlife from a jeep when we came upon a young wildebeest raked with claw marks standing away from the herd. Our guide commented that if we returned later it would be gone - eaten by a predator. Wildebeests are prey for many of the larger animals, just as rabbits are prey for desert predators.

I assume and hope the injured wildebeest and the baby bunny were both in a state of shock induced by their wounds. While nature is not kind, this may be one small way suffering is reduced for animals who are the prey instead of the predator.

Karnac, as a domesticated cat, is still a born predator in spite of the fact she receives all the food she can eat from a can and doesn't need to kill in order to survive. She is a perfect example of two opposite extremes. Karnac can stalk and hunt and play cruelly with a terrified mouse or injured bird, as well as purr and rub lovingly against my leg. When I am outside, she leaves her cozy napping place and follows me around the yard like a puppy.

Her benign, friendly presence completely masks the instinct she harbors deep within that gives her the capacity to kill. She reminds me that if I want to enjoy a furry little animal curled up in my lap, its small, warm purring body pressed against mine, then I have also to live with the other side of a cat's behavior, its predatory instinct. She also reminds me that if I want to live with and enjoy nature around me, then I will also have to witness some of nature's unpleasant realities.

At times I wish I knew what is in Karnac's mind. I think of a friend who taught at a foreign language school. One day she asked her five-year old son which foreign language he would like to learn. Expecting an answer like French, Spanish or German, his mother waited patiently while he thought it over. Finally, having decided, he answered confidently, "Cat." I think he was right. I would also like to learn cat language.

We inherited Karnac. She came with the house and

Unharmed baby Desert Cottontail – eats grasses, mesquite and cactus

in the beginning was not particularly friendly or affectionate. Since she was used to being outdoors and mostly fending for herself, it took over a year for her to want to come inside and to begin following us around the yard. Now she often comes with me and Geronimo when we go for walks around the ranch. She trots along a few steps behind and sometimes takes a shortcut through the creosote bushes. It seems a long walk for a little kitty, but she chooses to do it.

Sometimes I think of how Karnac and I are alike. I don't need to hunt or kill for my food and and neither does Karnac. But she still "plays" with a mouse and has no concept of the intense terror the mouse is going through.

In somewhat the same sense, I know I have at times used words that injured and left raw wounds in the mind of another person. I never mean to hurt anyone, but interpretations vary and what I think is play- ful or funny may be hurtful to someone who takes it seriously. The worst part is that, even if I dis- cover what I have done, I can't undo it because apologizing or "taking it back" can never erase the total damage. A residue of pain remains.

Cat nature is pretty well set, but human nature can change. The older I get, the more compassion I gain and the harder I try to under- stand others. But even then, should the need arise, the struggle for survival pops up and dominates and then I instinctively pounce, even though I regret it later. So, as my cat learned to love and trust me, I, also am learning that

more purring and less pouncing would benefit my relationships with others. Maybe I am learning cat language after all.

baby bunny in hands

> "Reverence for life is the ethic of love expanded to embrace the universe."
>
> - Albert Schweitzer

Coyote the Trickster

The coyote lopes along through dry brush and faded winter grasses. Only the top of her back and pointed ear tips give her away as she heads towards a higher ridge covered with dense clusters of old mesquite and creosote. I don't know what mission she is on, but mine is to check out a possible coyote den site which may belong to her. As I stand quietly and watch her move away, she pauses, looks in my direction, then hastens on towards higher ground.

Encouraged by her presence, I continue in the direction I've been given by our ranch foreman. It was yesterday morning when he told me I might like to look at a coyote den he'd discovered. Always interested in wildlife on the ranch, I get directions from him and set out this morning with my camera to take photographs of the new den.

Geronimo, forever excited and exuberant about a walk, has wandered off in a different direction following his nose as he searches for a tidbit of desert debris he can greedily ingest. Food is his main focus as we traipse the desert together.

One time he discovered a dead rabbit so desiccated it was nothing more than a cardboard-thin piece of leather. I tried to pry his jaws apart to pull out his precious serving of rabbit jerky, but he clamped his teeth down even tighter. He succeeded in carrying his prize home, head held high as if he had snagged the brass ring. I had to finish the walk with the stench of decomposed rabbit on my hands.

A small spot of bright blue catches my eye and I recognize it as the flag marker our foreman placed near the den so I could easily find it. Ordinarily I like my dog close to me, but today I'm glad he's wandered off. When he's at my side, he gets excited if I stop to examine a curiosity. He prances around and completely destroys the prints in the sand I'm trying to decipher.

Having found the den, I estimate the entrance to be about eighteen inches high and nine to twelve inches wide. In front of it is the mound of sand excavated from the burrow. I can't see far enough into the blackness of the opening to determine how deep or how far back the tunnel goes. I should have brought a flashlight, but even then I probably couldn't see to the end because of the bend in the passageway.

The opening is certainly coyote size, but I'm puzzled by the lack of prints in the sand. It's March, the right time of year for a litter of pups, but there would have to be evidence of adults coming and going. Coyotes scent mark their den areas with both urine and scat as a defensive measure and a warning. Sometimes rabbit fur, snake scales or other indigestible remnants are obvious in the scat.

While there are tracks nearby, the sand at the opening is smooth as if no one has recently gone in or out and the den opening seems too clean. But I have to remember, one overnight wind is enough to scour the sand free of all prints.

Something pulls my eyes to the distance where the coyote once again appears within my sight. She stands still and poised, looking in my direction. Then, in a second she disappears into the protective brush. I wonder, *Is this her den? Did she prepare it for her pups which may soon be due? Have I destroyed her secure nest by being here?*

With the lack of tracks or scat, I have to think this burrow is not being used at the moment. Once humans disturb a den, the parents are likely to move the pups away for safety. It's possible the female already had her babies here, but moved them after our foreman discovered the hole, left his foot prints and marker flag.

Coyote observing from a distance

Both male and female help to feed and raise the young, and sometimes yearlings stay around and even contribute to the parenting of the next year's litter. Coyotes (Canis latrans) usually live in small packs, but some are solitary.

The coyote I saw this morning could even be a lone male who just happened to be near the den site but has no connection to it. On trying to figure out what is going on with this den, I am left with an intriguing mystery, another secret the desert has not yet revealed.

In their natural habitat, it would be difficult to get close to a coyote. They keep their distance. But as we have taken more and more of their territory, stories appear of coyotes snatching cats, little dogs and even attacking small children.

While generally they are not a threat to man, anywhere a wild animal must hunt for food and easy prey appears, the animal will follow its nature, whether the victim is a pet cat or a defenseless young child.

A lot of coyote behavior is centered around food gathering. Studies have shown coyotes can prosper in urban areas because they are so good at scavenging. Open garbage cans and outside pet feeding dishes are easy sources for them.

One study of an urban area with numerous vacant lots showed how coyotes lived in the town, had pups in overgrown fields, yet ate much the same diet of mice, rats and vegetable material as they would have in the wild.

Eating rats and mice seems like a rather nice service coyotes perform. In heavily built up towns, however, they live almost entirely on garbage. Smart, stealthy and adaptable, they tend to stay away from people even while living in close proximity.

In urban areas people do lose small pets to coyotes. I think that was the fate of one cat, Belle Star, I had when I lived near the beach. But I have to remember that we moved in on coyote territory, they did not move in on ours.

As we continue to expand and build upon open land, we also inherit the creatures who naturally live there. I find it

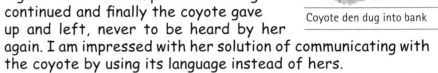

Coyote den dug into bank

encouraging to know they adapt and survive in spite of our encroachment. As they have learned to live with us, we need to learn how to live with them.

A friend living on the East Coast told me how she related to a coyote. One night she heard howling outside of her house. Not really wanting a coyote so close to her home, she went outside and in her loudest voice "howled" back. The coyote called louder and she raised her "volume" to a higher level. The competitive howling continued and finally the coyote gave up and left, never to be heard by her again. I am impressed with her solution of communicating with the coyote by using its language instead of hers.

My husband, Court, who is very logical and practical, describes his close-up coyote experience with an enthusiasm unusual for him. A few years ago, while walking the dog through a park, he rounded a bend in the path and found himself face to face with a coyote.

With less then fifteen feet between them, my husband, dog and coyote all stopped and viewed one another in silence. Then the coyote sat and the dog sat. The silence, my husband said later, seemed to last for an eternity, although it probably wasn't more than a minute or two. Finally the coyote stood, turned and trotted away. My husband exhaled, the dog stood up and they continued their walk as if nothing had happened.

Yet, Court says, that moment of quiet contemplation between coyote and man and dog left him with a reverence so strong he couldn't put it into words. This kind of magnetism between man and coyote is a fairly common experience. I don't know how to explain it or what name to give it. It is enough that it exists.

The cunning coyote is an intriguing animal. Perhaps it is the strong resemblance to the household dog that captures our fancy. Our loving attachments to our pets may be the basis for our attraction to a wild animal that seems so similar. It is not too different from the way I felt when dolphins appeared off shore on my morning beach walks. An invisible band seemed to bind me to them in a way I could only describe as irresistible.

Coyotes make their contribution to the mystique of the desert by their stealthy ways and nighttime high-pitched yipping sessions. They can appear like ghosts out of nowhere and disappear in an instant. On the ranch, we see them now and then in the early morning or at dusk, but they always see us first and keep their distance.

A recent coyote sighting report from my daughter had me wondering about her sanity. She and a friend said they'd seen a skinny, mangy-looking creature about the size of a small coyote. It was so pitiful in appearance, they named it Baby.

Over a period of a few months, Baby showed up numerous times, but always too far away to provide a really good look. My daughter, having lived in Texas for a number of years remembered stories Texans told of a strange creature they called a *chupacabra* It was coyote-like, but without hair and with an enlarged head. She decided a *chupacabra* had shown up here at the ranch. I laughed and went along with the idea for the fun of it. Another desert mystery, I thought.

A few weeks later, an article appeared in the newspaper reporting the capture and killing of a *chupacabra* in Texas. It's DNA would be analyzed to determine what animal it was. So I began to take the *chupacabra* story seriously, especially when our Hispanic neighbors across the road reported to our ranch foreman a *chupacabra* was stealing their dog food.

Several months went by and a follow-up news story reported the analyzed DNA of the *chupacabra* was entirely coyote. Apparently, some kind of disease causes the hair loss,

dark color of the hide and enlarged head. So *chupacabras* do exist, but they are not a strange animal, just a very sad and deformed coyote.

In Native American lore, Coyote is the trickster as well as the wise one. In most stories he outwits Raven and the other animals. Coyotes outwit us on our ranch. Fences don't keep them out. One time my daughter saw a coyote climb into a tree, something I would have thought impossible. She watched as it used the lower branches like rungs on a ladder to scamper upward.

Mostly nocturnal, their escapades take place at night. This is when they chew holes in our irrigation hoses. We have numerous ponds of fresh water for drinking, so it is not because they are thirsty. The theory is that they hear the trickling of water in the hose and interpret it as the squeaking of a mouse. So they bite the hose to get at what they think is prey.

One coyote who appeared in our back yard at dusk I found difficult to chase off. Even though Geronimo, who was probably twice as large, barked with his most menacing tone, the coyote held its ground. Since it refused to leave, I went running toward it clapping my hands and shouting. Still it only backed away a little and I had to go farther and farther from the house to chase it. Geronimo, with noisy growling, backed me up. Somehow I'd always envisioned Geronimo would be the aggressor and I would back him up. Oh well, at least now I know.

This may have been an example of a technique coyotes are known for. The pack sends out a decoy to lure a pet dog from the safety of its home, and when far enough away, the waiting pack attacks. Geronimo is smart enough or cowardly enough, I don't know which, to never go too far from our house.

I, on the other hand, have fewer instinctive "smarts." I had to observe the coyotes at work trying to entice my daughter's dog, Yolie, to where the pack waited before I understood their intentions. Yolie, a ranch dog, feels it's her duty to chaise rabbits and coyotes and she's wise enough to avoid coyote tricks.

Surprisingly, our most perceptive coyote guard is Karnak, the outside cat, who also sleeps on our bed the nights she decides to stay in. She has the uncanny ability of sensing a nearby coyote long before the dog or I see it. When she freezes in place with fur standing on end, tail flipping from side to side, I know there's a coyote around. Her powers of detection have kept her safe, and that is why we can allow her to be outside when she chooses.

I'm not afraid of coyotes. Just as with domesticated dogs, who bite when threatened, safety comes with not playing the role of victim. Animals in the wild attack when they sense a weak target. They need to conserve their energy, and therefore are careful about choosing their prey. The coyotes I get a glimpse of here in the desert are a part of the balance of nature. Without them the rabbit population would expand to unmanageable numbers.

As I leave the coyote den site, still puzzled with the mystery of a perfectly dug hole with a coyote near by and yet little evidence of activity, I make a mental note to return in a few days to see if there is any change. I may never solve this mystery, but it is the trying that stimulates and excites me.

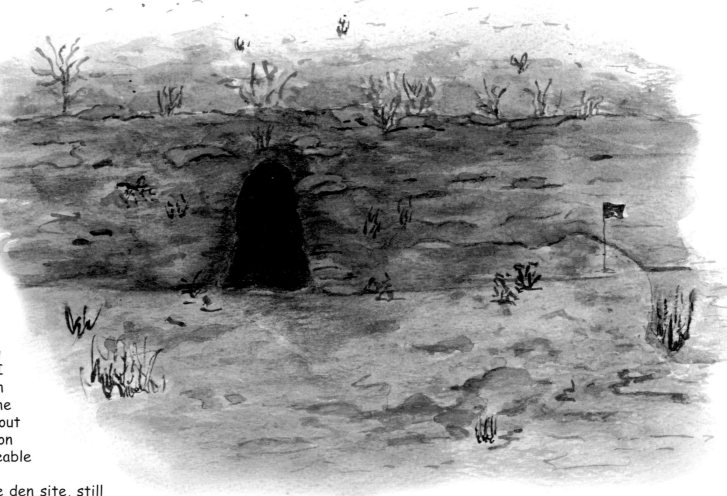

Empty coyote den

"The cunning coyote is an intriguing animal. Perhaps it is the strong resemblance to the household dog that captures our fancy."

"- one intrepid climber discovers that sometimes the
journey is the destination..."

- Robert Earle Howells

Mushroom Mystery

Winter weather in the desert fades into milder nights and warmer days. By mid-morning the sun bears down with brutal intensity. I've been out walking for several hours, poking under bushes to identify burrow holes of small nocturnal animals. Since I don't get to see these creatures during daylight hours, I'm hopeful that in time I will be able to recognize the type of animal who lives in the burrow by the shape and location of the entrance.

So far I haven't been very successful. Most holes look much the same except for a variation in size. My dog, Geronimo, isn't any help as he bounds ahead, his nose alert for sniffing around shrubs and in crannies for something only he is privy to. I decide to give it up for today and head home across the wash.

Ahead of me, on a stretch of flat gravel, a strange moon-like landscape stops me short. Little growths I don't recognize poke up from the sand and I think. *Are those mushrooms or is the glare of the sun distorting my vision?*

I've walked this area for over four years and never before seen anything like these curious objects that look like rolled up wads of tissue paper on stems. I count nineteen of the shaggy ghost-like plants. Some are about three inches high, others as tall as eight. Mushrooms in the dry desert? I always thought they only grew in moist places. This is a new mystery.

I kneel in the sand to examine the bizarre-looking white shoots and pull one out of the ground to examine more closely. It has the same elongated shape as the caramel-colored, highly-prized morels we used to pick in the Minnesota woods.

I have fond memories of following my dad and brothers into the forest where we searched around trees in the fecund leaf mold for the treasured growths. I was only a little kid, but I still remember carrying them home in a basket, my mouth already anticipating the earthy taste of freshly-picked mushrooms pan-fried in butter.

Geronimo thinks I've stopped to give him a doggie cookie. He prances around the mushroom bed in anticipation of his treat and knocks over several of the delicate plants before I can call him away. To him, every gross, icky thing is food, but I'm relieved he's shown no interest in eating them, because these mushrooms look weird enough to be poisonous.

I have no idea if the one in my hand could kill me, is deliciously edible or something in between. It has a base, stem and oval cap like a child's drawing of a pine tree. As I squeeze it between my fingers, I feel the same firm, but softly-yielding texture of the mushrooms I buy at the grocery store.

Placing the specimen in a plastic bag to take back to the house for further study, frees my hands to take pictures of the mushroom patch before I head for home with Geronimo loping ahead, still hoping for the dog biscuit he knows I have in my pocket.

Field of 6 to 8 inch-high Desert Inky Caps

Back at the house I begin by checking in the book I call my desert bible, an *Audubon Society Nature Guide* entitled *Deserts*. The color plates in this book are especially helpful for identifying much of what I see on my desert walks. I don't actually expect mushrooms to be in the book and am pleasantly surprised to find three different species pictured.

The Desert Inky Cap *(Podaxis pistillaris)* matches my morning discovery. I learn it can be found in the Sonoran and Mojave Deserts as well as the Great Basin. At a maximum height of twelve inches it seems huge for a fungus.

The name, inky cap, derives from an autodigestion process that occurs as the young white cap matures and turns black. It's not a mushroom to eat and shouldn't be mistaken for another inky cap *(Coprinus comatus)*, the popular edible species not found in the desert, which underscores why Latin names are so important.

Common names are often regional, confusing and nonspecific. These two look-alike mushroom species, one edible and one not, are also a good reason to avoid eating any wild mushroom unless you are an expert at identification. Even though we collected them in the wild when I was little, I wouldn't dream of doing it today because I don't know enough for it to be safe.

Mushrooms are fast-growing and their form can change hourly so identification by sight can be tricky, but the fact that they spring up after a rain explains part of their mysterious appearance in the desert wash where I came upon them so unexpectedly.

The type of organic material or humus that supports their growth remains unknown to me, but I can guess it was deposited in the sand after recent rains sent debris-laden water gushing through the area.

However, several weeks later, I find two Desert Inky Caps pushed up through the compacted material in the middle of our road. How did organic matter to support inky caps filter through a rock-hard asphalt road surface? So the mystery deepens and I realize the desert will not reveal its secrets so easily.

Finding from further research that mushrooms don't have roots, begins to help explain the mushrooms in the road. Instead of a seed pushing roots downward into soil, mushrooms evolve from tiny filaments intertwined in a branching mass called a mycelium which grows in organic matter. This is the vegetative part of the plant.

The above-ground growth we see is really the plant's fruit. Its purpose is to produce enough spores to find a suitable environment and ensure the plant's survival. Even though the middle of a hard-packed, dusty, oiled road doesn't seem like a good growing area, I can at least understand how a portion of organic matter deposited there could support a mushroom.

Nature knows what it's doing, but sometimes I think even nature gets a little weird. I remain in awe and accept the miracles that are mysteries to me, but if I can better understand how nature operates, my world becomes just a bit brighter.

Of the 70,000 species of fungi in the world, perhaps it's not so strange to find that several species exist in the desert. The Buried-stalk Puffball *(Tulostoma simulans)* is another variety I see occasionally. Its round ball top is the spore sac that falls apart at maturity to release the spores. In the ones I have seen, the stalk has always been buried in the sand.

Mysteries and strange adaptations seem to be the norm for the desert, but mushrooms throughout the world have their own category of weirdness. The legendary red *Amanita muscaria* is an example of how unusual natural forms influence folklore and play a role in many accepted traditions.

Amanita muscaria is dangerously toxic

Mushroom Christmas ornament of silvered glass from early 1900's.

to humans, but only hallucinogenic to Lapland reindeer who find it irresistible and seek it out. The reindeer in their "high-flying" state may be the basis for the idea of flying reindeer pulling a sleigh.

In Germany, this mushroom was pictured on 19th century Christmas cards and is often seen in children's books. Mushroom-shaped glass Christmas ornaments are still available from Germany, and Santa's coat of red and white may have derived from the mushroom's red cap with raised white spots. All this from a mere mushroom.

Maybe the strange white fungi I found growing in the wash and in the road are just another of the oddities the desert tosses out to tease and capture the attention of those who explore desert fact and lore. As examples of another mystery I can't fully explain, they remind me I have much to learn. As time passes and I spend more time in the desert, some of my questions will be answered, but meanwhile many adaptations to the harsh, dry climate appear bizarre and improbable.

Perhaps it's the lure of mysteries and desert weirdness that draws me, in the same way a good mystery novel captures my attention and won't release me until the puzzle is solved. So each new discovery I make adds to the picture and I am struck with the enormity of it all.

I realize I am like a newborn, just beginning my journey of knowledge. I can never know all I want to. The best I can do is to continue seeking and be happy with each new acquaintance along the way. There will be pauses and resting places in my travels, but once I stop asking questions, stop learning new things and cease wanting to solve mysteries, that is when I will stop growing.

Buried-stalk Puffball, 2 inches high. Stalks often covered with blow sand.

"When discovery no longer matters, and existence becomes my only goal, that is the time my effective life will be over. Until then each new thing I learn is an irregularly-shaped piece that helps fill in the puzzle of my life."

Puffball split open to release spores

"Let nature be your teacher."

- William Wordsworth

Cochineal

After a brief walk in dry 70 degree air at sunup, I return to the house for breakfast in the garden. While the coffee brews, I go outside to water a few plants during the cool of the morning. With nozzle in hand, I drag the long hose around the side of the house and past a large prickly pear cactus covered with tiny white puffs. It looks as if a roll of cotton exploded and snowed on the plant.

The spots are actually cochineal bugs and will ultimately kill the cactus if I don't remove them. I aim a strong jet of water at the cactus paddles. The white, fuzzy-appearing spots loosen and wash onto the ground. Those that are crushed by the force of the water leave a burst of red residue on the sand.

If I didn't know better, I would think the reddish-purple color was blood from the crushed insects. But, from my trips to Mexico, I've learned it's the insect itself that turns red, not its blood.

The cochineal *(Dactylopius coccus)* beetle is a scale insect common throughout the American Southwest and Mexico. If not removed, the bugs will multiply and feed on the plant's juices until the cactus finally dies. But the bugs have a use as well. In Mexico, cactus infected with cochineal (coach-en-ee-ah) is cultivated for the exceptionally fine red dye made from the insects.

It was in Oaxaca, Mexico, on a museum field trip I first learned about cochineal dye. Any rug or fabric made with dye from the cochineal beetle is expensive compared with those made with commercial dyes, and when the dye-making process was explained to me I understood why.

The beetles are scraped from the cactus, immersed in hot water, dried in the sun and crushed into powder, which sounded fine until I found out that it takes 150,000 beetles to produce one kilogram (approx. 2.2 lbs.) of dye. My neglected prickly pear, covered with bugs might yield a half teaspoon of dye. So it is easy to see that this dye-making process involves a huge amount of hand work and was

cochineal-dyed rug

seldom used after commercial dyes became available.

Because red is a common color today, I sometimes forget it was so highly prized by ancient civilizations that it was reserved for the elite and sometimes considered more precious than gold. When the Aztecs needed red, it came from fuzzy white cochineal insects thriving on prickly pear cactus.

Even though the Spaniards ravished Mexico to loot the fabled gold of the Aztecs and Mayans, red cochineal dye was the first product to be exported from South America after the Spanish conquest.

The dye became famous for its brilliant red color and found its way around the globe and back to the new world. That was how the British achieved the distinctive red coats worn by their soldiers during the Revolutionary War, by using cochineal dye from Mexico.

Today, after an era when synthetic dyes were used for their convenience and low price, the value of this natural coloring has returned as a desirable element. In Mexico, Zapotec weavers are producing high-quality handwoven rugs and fabrics utilizing dye derived from cochineal insects. Plantations of prickly pear heavily infested with the bug have become viable as businesses and are cultivated expressly for dye making.

If prickly pear cactus were not already an exotic plant for harboring insects that change from white to intense red when crushed, it would still be special because of its many food, medicinal and ornamental uses.

While I prize prickly pears for their intensely colored flowers and the bold statement their presence makes in the garden, in Mexico and South America several varieties of prickly pear are harvested for food, the making of candy and a natural medicine for diabetes.

When the bright yellow flowers, fushia in some varieties, fade, hard green fruits develop. Slowly they become soft, turn orange, then red when ripe. The flesh of the fruit is fifteen percent sugar, melon textured and peppered with small black seeds. Often used for jams and jellies, the taste is similar to kiwi fruit.

The first time I saw a display of *nopales* in a grocery store, I had no idea what they were. It wasn't until I learned the entire prickly pear plant is called *nopal* that I realized *nopales* are cactus pads. The most tender new parts used for making stews and pickles are *nopalitos*. The red fruits that develop after the flowers bloom are *tunas*. I have been treated to tasting these natural

Yellow blooming cactus

foods and they are quite appealing, but I haven't yet experimented with cooking them.

Native desert people collected prickly pear pads, fruits and flowers to add to their food source. They used a stick to break off fruits and cactus joints, then rubbed them in the sand to remove the tiny spines called glochids. Sometimes spines and glochids were burned off.

To me, tiny barbed glochids are more of a danger than cactus spines because they are so hard to see, often as small as a hair, and easy to touch. Once lodged in skin, their barbed tips go deeper and deeper with movement. Sometimes they itch, other times their prick feels as sharp as a needle.

The common beavertail cactus *(Opuntia basilaris),* a type of prickly pear that grows wild in the Sonoran Desert, has glochids instead of spines and I am positive it attacks me as I take my walks. I often end up with them stuck in my hand or leg and they are almost impossible to completely pluck out. There are always one or two I can't find that plague me for days. The craziness is that I would never touch a beavertail. Yet I seem to pick up glochids from somewhere. I've decided the beavertails set glochid traps I fall into.

Once on a trip to Monterey, Mexico, with archaeologist, Professor Carlos Villarreal, to view petroglyphs or rock art, I stumbled on

Dried cactus bloom and pod – not the edible kind

a rocky slope and fell with one arm landing in a cactus bed. When I pulled myself up with my free hand, I had a whole cactus joint at least a foot long pinned to my other arm. My husband and daughter just looked at me with horror and pity. They had no idea what to do about all those spines puncturing my skin, pinning the cactus on to me like a clinging child.

Professor Villarreal, who lived and worked in the area, picked up a stick and before I knew what had happened, whipped the spiny stem off my arm. I was free of the big piece, but not yet in the clear. The cactus bed I had fallen into had plants with both spines and glochids.

During the ride back to town in the truck bed of the archaeologist's pickup over rough and dusty gravel roads, I had to hold my glochid-covered arm away from my body for the entire two hours it took to return to Professor Villarreal's home.

For the next hour or so, while everyone else rested and drank tea, I sat in a straight-backed chair while the professor's wife used a small tweezers to pull glochids from my arm, palm, fingers and back of my hand. Having done this for her husband many times, she got most of them. But since they are so small as to be almost invisible, for weeks afterward at odd times I experienced the unwelcome, somewhat painful prick of a missed glochid.

It makes me shudder and itch just to think about it. I can't imagine what it must have been like for a pioneer woman or a cowboy or any other early inhabitant who may have had the same experience, but without the aid of a handy tweezers.

Early Europeans and Asians didn't have to deal with cactus spines since cacti as a group are New World plants originating primarily throughout the American Southwest and South America. Spines, by the way, are not the defining characteristic of the cactus family; it is aeroles, those regularly placed spots on the stems from which spines or glochids emanate that distinguish cactus from other plant families.

During the era when botanical gardens were popular on estates of wealthy Europeans, unusual varieties of cactus were collected and highly prized. Perfectly suited to the arid desert, instead of the cold English countryside, they had to be coddled in greenhouses with warmth and light, which added to their exotic appeal.

When I first moved to the desert, cactus plants seemed strange and foreign to me and I bought numerous books identifying the multitude of different varieties. Little did I know that only a few are common in our Sonoran Desert and those are easily identified.

Neither did it occur to me that cactus might also be an edible plant, but I have learned a lot during my years of desert living. The plants and animals with their adaptations to heat and lack of regular water have become an inspiration I use for myself. Not that I try to live without water or stay out in excessive heat, but that I do understand the human body and soul are capable of making changes and living in harmony within many environments, both mental and physical.

The prickly pear in my garden, now free of its fuzzy white cochineal decorations, has a chance to recover and grow into a large specimen if I can keep it bug free. I remind myself to check it more often so the little beasties won't have a chance to take over again.

The appealing scent of fresh coffee I began brewing earlier interrupts my musings, and I abandon my watering job for breakfast in the garden. Being quiet and surrounded by nature in a landscape where survival is based on making unique adaptations to existing conditions is enough for me this morning.

"Like Scarlet O'Hara in *Gone With the Wind*, I'll think about the rest tomorrow."

"The prickly pear in my garden, now free of its fuzzy white cochineal decorations, has a chance to recover and grow into a large specimen."

Beavertail cactus – has tiny glochids on pads, edible fruits called *tunas*.

"Hope is the thing with feathers that perches in the soul"

- Emily Dickinson

Vandalizing Birds

The first time I saw the nest was at sunset. A red crystal sun mounted in a metallic sky of gold slowly settled below the horizon leaving behind purple rays stretching like arms into the firmament. Against such a magnificent backdrop, a small brown ball dangling from a tree limb caught my attention. I could see it plainly through the glass panes in the French doors of my office.

Verdin *(Auriparus flaviceps)*
4 - 4 ½ inches, feeds on insects, seeds, berries

Not more than five feet away, a finely woven nest of small twigs and plant fibers dangled from an over-hanging palo verde branch. *How long has that been there,* I remember thinking at the time, *and why haven't I noticed it before?*

I was curious about the nest. Even though the branch it hung on was low in the tree, it remained above my head, too high to do more than look at from below.

The next morning, as I worked at my desk, I found myself totally distracted by two small gray birds with yellowish heads hopping from branch to branch twittering and chirping. Slowly, from a far limb of the tree, they worked their way closer and closer to the nest until finally one of the birds popped out of sight into the side of the globular mass. It was then I realized this bird's home was constructed as a hollow ball with a side entrance. I was fascinated. Never before had I seen this type of nest.

I continued to watch the other bird perched close by. Its yellow head highlighted in the morning sunlight, was the characteristic I used for identification in looking up the species in my *Field Guide to Western Birds.* Verdins *(Auriparus flaviceps),* I found, are true desert dwellers living in brushy, arid lands.

While most birds belong to a family of other birds with some similar characteristics, verdins, I discovered, are not closely related to any other bird in the western hemisphere. They thrive in the low desert containing mesquite, creosote and other taller shrubs.

Primarily insect eaters, which makes them automatic winners in my mind, they also take nectar from flowers and have even been known to come to hummingbird feeders for sugar water. They flit around much like the common chickadee, are desert colored, desert adapted and a delight to have in my yard.

That spring I continued to keep track of the the verdin couple with their nest hanging where I could so easily see it. After a while I began to recognize their particular chirping which alerted me they were nearby.

Their peculiar way of dancing around from limb to limb before entering the nest continued as their behavior pattern. Wary and watchful, they ducked into the side entrance of the ball of sticks only after checking carefully to be sure there was no danger. In my research, I found that the birds sleep in the nest at night as well as use it to raise their young, so it really functions as their home.

All spring I checked periodically and happily watched the verdins. Hoping to catch a glimpse of their babies, I kept my binoculars handy to get a close up view, should I spot a hatchling. The two adults entered the nest ball with insects in their beaks, so I know they were feeding their young, but not once did I catch sight of a baby bird.

The next February, as I sat working at my office desk, occasionally looking out at the courtyard and the palo verde tree, the verdins again entertained me with the same evasive tactics used before in entering the old nest built the previous year. A few repairs were made, and the ball of twigs and plant fibers appeared good as new.

This time I plotted ways to look into the cozy bird home. I wanted to see the soft, downy lining I knew had to be there to cradle the greenish dotted eggs. I considered using a stepladder and an angled dentist's mirror, the little round one, he sticks into my mouth to see behind my teeth. I could insert it into the small side opening and see inside the ball of sticks.

But my plans never materialized. I decided not to chance frightening the birds into abandoning the nest. Once again I missed even so much as a glimpse of the young ones.

Now a third year has passed and March is upon us. I look out at the verdins' nest and am surprised to see a larger bird, not a verdin, pecking at the puff ball mass. The bird pulls twigs and pieces of nesting material from the sides and top. I watch in amazement and think, *I can't believe that bird is stealing material from the verdins' nest.*

Yet, as I continue to observe, the verdins perch near by and watch their home being torn apart twig by twig, fiber by fiber. Occasionally there is a small fracas, as the verdins flit noisily around the nest and dive at the marauding intruders, but the vandalizing continues.

I cannot identify the ones doing the stealing, but they look much like sparrows. "Little brown bird" is a phrase used in birding groups for all of those indistinct and hard to identify birds, so I will call the intruders, little brown birds. Whoever they are, I wish they'd go away and leave the verdins at peace. In a few days, the branch is bare, all remnants of a nest are gone.

I keep hoping to see the verdins rebuild, but there is no sign of them. I feel abandoned and empty. When I moved to the desert, the verdins were one of my early discoveries. I think of them as a welcoming committee. They entertained me and gave me a glimpse of how desert birds differ from coastal varieties. It is as if I discovered a new species and it became extinct before I really got to know it.

The days go by and the palo verde tree dresses itself in bright yellow spring blossoms. It makes me miss the yellow-headed verdins even more and I long to see again their round twiggy nest with the side entrance. I feel especially sorry they were driven away and a little guilty because I couldn't protect them.

Aggressive bird behavior taking advantage of weaker birds is too close to some human behaviors. There are bullies in all societies, but I didn't expect to witness bird bullies right outside my window. Certainly there are plenty of twigs in the desert for all birds. Why pull apart another's nest to gather what is readily available?

TYPICAL FLIGHT FEATHER

RACHIS

BARB

CALAMUS

sunlight creeping through the leaves of a mesquite tree. A round twiggy ball dangles near the end of a far branch.

So, the verdins are back. They have a new nest, but in a different tree. Bird or man, we repair and we rebuild. Challenges are met and life continues. The verdins will tend their new nest, lay some eggs, raise their young.

I will go on discovering new insights as well as idiosyncrasies inherent in the desert. The vandalizing birds are probably not suffering from serious conscience issues, but I certainly hope people with nothing better to do than harm others will regret their actions at some time within their life's journey. I can only feel sorry for the destroyers, and be thankful my life is aimed at building rather than tearing down.

Perhaps it was just plain laziness, like the cowbird who lays its eggs in nests of another species and lets stepparents rear its young. I guess I'll never be able to figure out bird vandalizing behavior any better than people vandalizing behavior.

This week someone deliberately drove a truck into our back gate, flattening it to the ground. We think they wanted to steal a tractor parked just inside the property. However, they couldn't drive the tractor away since it was only there because it had broken down and we hadn't yet had it repaired. The vandalism of the gate cost a good deal of money for repairs and took time that could have been used more productively. In a perfect world we wouldn't need a gate.

This morning, as I leave the house for my walk, I decide to go in a different direction. As I pass by my husband's office window, I glance up to follow a dusky ray of morning

"The truth is that life is delicious, horrible, charming, frightful, sweet, bitter, and that is everything."

- Anatole France

Dangling Snake

Yesterday, while walking in the lower palm field, I caught a glimpse of one of our resident roadrunners with a long skinny thing dangling from its beak. Straining for a better look as the bird rounded the far side of a creosote bush, I could see it had about ten inches of snake hanging from its mouth. I had hoped for an even closer look to satisfy my fascination tinged with revulsion at the thought of a half-swallowed snake. But the roadrunner scooted off into the desert brush and I lost sight of it.

As I rested in the shade of a rambling mesquite tree, I couldn't get the image of a snake, half consumed with the rest dangling free, out of my mind. I had to swallow hard to hold back the gagging sensation I felt in my throat.

Small rattlesnakes are part of a roadrunner's normal diet along with scorpions, cockroaches and black widow spiders. Certainly not my idea of gourmet food, but I'm glad roadrunners like these creatures generally considered obnoxious by most people.

The pair of roadrunners claiming my yard as their territory serve as an efficient bug and reptile control. It makes me feel much safer around my house and yard knowing there is little likelihood I will inadvertently stumble upon a rattlesnake as I work in my garden and putter around plants and paths.

So far not one rattlesnake has shown itself on our property, either near the house or anywhere on our hundred acres.

I don't deny they exist here, I just haven't seen them. Once one of the ranch hands came upon an injured rattler on the southern edge of our land, nowhere near the house. Since it had numerous wounds, probably from an attack by an animal or bird, he killed it and, knowing of my interest in nature, saved the rattles and skin for me.

I came home that day to find a shredded rattlesnake skin hanging over a rib of the shade umbrella on the back patio. I wasn't too excited about having a snake skin dangling over my patio table, but I appreciated the thought. It reminded me of my cat who sometimes brings a dead mouse to the kitchen door as a gift.

Roadrunner with partially-swallowed snake

In my research on roadrunners, I found it is not uncommon for them to eat snakes. However, they often can't swallow a whole snake at one time. So they swallow as much as they can and the rest just hangs out of their beak until the part in their stomach is digested to make room for the next portion.

When I think about a string of food half in my stomach digesting, with the rest stuck in my throat hanging out of my mouth, the idea is about as sickening as I can imagine. I know it shouldn't bother me. After all, I'm not a roadrunner, but I do have a tendency to identify with or impart human characteristics to wildlife.

Just as I am feeling smug at not having gross eating habits like roadrunners, I find an article in the newspaper reporting on how each of us as human beings eats a pound or more of dirt in a lifetime, probably several pounds if we live to old age. How does that happen, and if I'm not aware of each small morsel mixed with my food, does it really matter?

It turns out that common dirt, or typical soil, won't hurt us. But what bothers me is the list of other things allowed in our food by the FDA. Fifty grams of cornmeal, for example, passes inspection unless it contains one or more whole insects, fifty or more insect fragments, two or more rodent hairs, and one or more rodent excreta.

In a can of peaches, just under three percent of the fruit is allowed to be moldy or wormy. With canned mushrooms, an

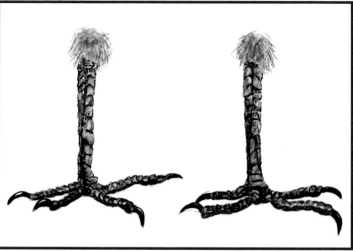

Roadrunners are unusual in that two toes point forward and two backward. Most birds have three toes forward and only one in back that touches the ground.

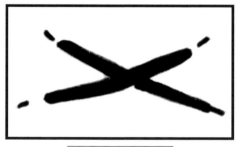

Roadrunner footprint

average twenty or more maggots per one hundred grams condemns the product to the trash pile. Here's where I draw the line, I really don't want any maggots in my mushrooms. Although I admit if I don't know they're there and they don't hurt me, why should I care?

These small amounts of contamination are allowed because they are of no danger healthwise. They contribute or detract mainly to the aesthetic quality of the food. Obviously these numbers must work out so that the allowed items are so small they are not apparent when we open a can of fruit or mushrooms. At least I've never seen any of these gross things in my food. Ground or chopped up, I guess I wouldn't notice.

Then, as I'm feeling a bit squeamish about what is allowed in the food we buy, I discover there are numerous countries including Vietnam, Cambodia, China and Mexico where bugs are an accepted part of people's diets. With a protein content as much as twice that of beef, bugs are a cheap and available food source.

In Mexico, fried green caterpillars are called *cuchama*, at other times they are boiled with a little lime. Spicy locusts, ant eggs and maguey worms are showing up as exotic fare at expensive restaurants, and clear candy with a bug inside is made for children. However distasteful this may sound, it is far better nutritionally than the sugary sodas and high-fat fast food we allow our children to eat in the United States.

There is even a movement in Mexico to produce high-protein bug larvae powder for enriching tortillas and other foods. The best thing about gathering pest bugs for food is that it eliminates the use of pesticides for bug control. And in some rural areas farmers have found they can get more money for edible bugs than for their crops, plus they save the cost of expensive pesticides. Who would have guessed?

Even though I'm still not ready to eat bugs, I know I inadvertently consume dirt. Root vegetables such as celery, spinach and lettuce we buy at the grocery store frequently have dirt on them and washing them carefully doesn't always guarantee they are dirt free.

According to Jay Bell, a professor of soil science at Minnesota's College of Agriculture, dirt is not the same as soil. Soil is a living body that occurs on the surface of the earth. When it is removed from the earth's surface, it becomes dirt. Soil has many nutrients in it, but dirt no longer supports organic matter.

Darn, I was hoping there was some nutritional benefit to that pound of dirt I am apparently ingesting in insidious minute amounts that sneak into my food. I'm beginning to be very impressed that my digestive system can accept all sorts of items, use what it can and let the rest pass through. I'm also beginning to think the roadrunner's meal isn't so strange after all.

I had hoped to see the roadrunner with the snake again the next day and thereafter, so I could get some idea of how fast the snake was digested. Unfortunately, as hard as I searched on my morning walks, I never again saw the roadrunner with the dangling snake. So I have no idea of how long it ran around with part of the snake exposed.

I also don't know what kind of snake it was. If it was a rattlesnake, I'm glad the roadrunner won the confrontation. If it was a coachwhip or one of our other nonpoisonous, benign, rat-eating snake species, I am sorry, but I understand that is nature's way. Prey and predator have existed together since life began and will continue to vie for space in wild places. And sometimes we are privileged to witness their interaction.

Zebratail lizard 6 to 9 inches.
Roadrunners eat small lizards.

"Never doubt that a small group of thoughtful,
committed citizens can change the world: indeed,
its the only thing that ever has."

- Margaret Mead

Desert Glass

My morning walk begins as usual with my big dog trotting ahead down a well-worn trail I often take. But today I head overland toward Hidalgo Wash and Geronimo backtracks to correct his mistake. We cross a gradually-sloped hill studded with creosote, Mormon tea and indigo bush. Ahead lies the arroyo, defined by a river of sand snaking through clusters of smoke trees, aptly named because from a distance their gray-green foliage resembles hovering puffs of smoke. Scattered throughout the wash a few newly-rooted palo verde trees with green-colored bark struggle for water to continue their growth.

As I carefully pick my way down a steep slope to reach the bottom of the wash, small glints of light reflecting rays from the low morning sun flash from a patch of shattered glass on the gravelly hillside. At one time this serene natural area was littered with trash dumped here by people who neither appreciated nor respected the desert. While most of the offending debris has since been removed, there are places where small glass shards poke out of the sand and mar the natural landscape. When I come upon one of these areas, I feel compelled, in some way I can't explain, to remove the offending litter.

I begin picking up jagged remains of broken bottles, some with only an edge protruding from the sandy crust of the arroyo's sloping bank. One small sharp sliver punctures my thumb drawing a bubble of blood. As I blot it with

Fountain filled with beach glass shards

a piece of tissue from my pocket, my mind drifts back to the walks I took on the ocean beach and eagerly looked for beach glass in the damp sands of a coastal morning. How different it was then to rub my thumb over a fragment of green bottle glass, smoothed and polished by the sea, its sharp edges rounded to feel good in my hand.

Here in the desert, those same kinds of broken glass pieces retain their sharp edges and intrude upon the view as reminders of man's irresponsible use of the land. Instead of searching for the shards to collect them, as I did at the beach, I pick them up only to remove an eyesore from the otherwise pristine and wild desert.

Glass, as a man-made product, seems alien to the natural desert environment. Yet, glass is a product of the desert since its main ingredient is the quartz-laden sand covering the desert floor.

The manufacture of glass began in the deserts of Mesopotamia – now Iraq and Iran – around 1550 B.C. Three hundred years later, and about a century after the reign of Tutankhamen, a glass factory was in operation on the Nile delta in Egypt. From archaeological evidence we know that quartz sand was heated to its melting point, colorized and combined with plant ash to form valuable ingots shipped throughout the Mediterranean. From these early times and throughout history glass has been treasured and sought after. But in today's world of overabundance most glass, except for art glass, is utilitarian, a throw away item.

Glass is not only a manufactured item, it also

occurs naturally in the form of obsidian, a black glass much sought after in ancient times. Forged in the bowels of the earth, obsidian is formed when volcanoes throw out molten material and sudden cooling under low pressure takes place. Its chemical composition is much the same as granite, but granite results when cooling takes place slowly under great pressure. A vitreous rock, obsidian is hard and brittle, has a glassy appearance and is usually black, but gray, yellow and brown are possible.

It was highly valued and traded by early people. It could be knapped or flaked into sharp cutting tools, spear points and arrowheads. I didn't realize obsidian is actually glass until a friend who was skilled in flint knapping (shaping points and arrowheads by flaking off pieces to create a sharp cutting edge) gave me a gift of an arrowhead he'd fashioned from a piece of clear glass. It was exactly like an obsidian point except it was transparent instead of black.

The largest mass of obsidian known is Obsidian Cliff in Yellowstone National Park. When a road was needed at the foot of this mountain of natural glass, the engineers had to be creative. Since obsidian cannot be drilled or blasted like other rock, they had to treat it like glass. By building fires on it and dashing cold water on the hot surface, they caused it to shatter and make room for their project. There must have been some marvelous hunks of obsidian lying around after the road went through. I wonder where they are today.

Even the name obsidian has an interesting origin. Derived from a rock discovered in Ethiopia by Obsius, it was erroneously changed to Obsidius by Pliny. Therefore, the

rock became obsidian. Ancient Mexicans used it under the name *itzili*, and quarried it at *Cerro de las Navajas,* or Hill of Knives, near Timapan.

When I think of glass formed by cataclysmic events brought about by nature, I am reminded of a fictional story that fascinated me when I was a child. The plot centered around a group of scientists experimenting with massive forces capable of blowing up the earth. The residue left from their experimental explosions was a strange green-colored glass never before seen.

At the same time, a group of archaeologists worked to uncover the remnants of civilizations before their own. As they dug deeper and deeper, the artifacts they discovered were older and older, each representing a people more ancient than the layer above.

At last they uncovered the layer with relics of the most primitive of known civilizations, but they continued to dig down even deeper. Under all of the strata of human habitation they found one final layer. It consisted of a strange green-colored glass.

My young mind was so captivated by this little piece of science fiction that I never forgot it. So, as I pick up green and brown bottle glass from the sand today, I wonder how long these shards would survive intact if I left them in place. Eons from now, I expect they would be buried deep within the ever-changing, evolving crust covering earth.

Greater Roadrunner –
20-24 inches, member of the cuckoo family, can run at speed of up to 15 miles per hour

Whether they would have a message for future generations, I cannot know.

With a plastic grocery sack, so full of broken glass fragments I can hardly carry it, I return to the house and drop the bag of shards into one of our garbage cans. An edge of white plastic peeking out from behind a low wall near the trash bins reminds me that's where I stashed all of the sea glass I brought with me when we moved from the beach to the desert.

At that time I didn't have a chance to sort things. My husband groans when he remembers seeing the packers carefully wrapping in double paper everything from under the kitchen sink, including used scouring pads and almost empty bottles of detergent. So it was no surprise when one box I unpacked contained six plastic grocery bags filled with shards of beach glass from the glass garden I constructed at my former beach home.

Without a clue as to what I might do with beach glass in the desert, I stashed the bags out of sight where they collected dirt and served as a haven for bugs. Two winters, a few rain storms, lots of dry leaves and blowing dust left their mark on the fragile plastic filled with heavy glass. While not on my mind daily, I knew they were there and had to be dealt with at some time.

Today, after my morning of desert glass cleanup, seems perfect for tackling the beach glass collection. When I try to lift one of the bags to inspect its contents, the plastic, weakened from time and weather, falls apart in my hands.

I use a small shovel and pail to transport the pile of dirty glass pieces mixed with leaf debris and all kinds of winged and multi-legged creatures to the back patio area. I empty the pail onto the grass where our resident roadrunners come quickly to gobble up the crawling insects that emerge in hoards. I watch the bugs running frantically about looking for new hiding places and I feel as if I've stepped into a scene from a grade "B" horror film. I move back to give the roadrunners room to feast on the bugs.

So in the desert, what do I do with thousands of bits of sea-and sand-washed glass collected from the beach? As I pick up the dirty pieces and dip them in clear water, an idea strikes me. I will use the pale green, blue, brown and colorless glass as a substitute for water in the three-tiered Mexican fountain on the patio. The glass will function as a kind of mirage, like the ones we see on shimmering hot roads. It can simulate water without actually being water.

Softly colorful with a bit of sparkle, the beach glass now has a home in the desert from which its main ingredient, quartz, originated. Its raw material has come full circle.

As I compare beach glass with desert glass, one pleasing and sought after, the other merely litter, I realize this is another example I can apply to the way I live. I can use the irritations and annoyances of everyday life as a process to become more understanding and accepting, or I can let life's difficulties leave me with sharp edges and emotional wounds that don't heal. I have choices I can make. The lessons to be gleaned from common things continue to give me guidance as I go about my daily tasks.

Fremont's Pincushion, a flower often found growing at the base of a creosote bush.

"Observation more than books, experience rather
than persons are the prime educators."

- Amos Bronson Alcott

Nature's Drugstore

It's 6:35 in the morning. Slanting rays of warm sunlight mingle with the residue of cooler nighttime air still coating the ground. I breathe deeply enjoying the faint scent of fresh, crisp herbal spice. *Which plant*, I wonder, *is responsible for this pungent but pleasant smell ?* As I pass by a six-foot tall creosote bush, I pull one of its dark-green, leafy branches to my nose and sniff like a dog following a scent. The resinous, medicinal odor is so strong it triggers a sudden memory from my past.

I'm taken back to the drugstore in the Midwest where I worked after school when I was a teenager. In those days, drugstores had a pervading medicinal odor. Whether it was from a particular tonic in use then, or from a variety of remedies dispensed from large containers into small bottles, I do not know. But the smell, so like the creosote bush, comes back to me as distinct as if I were standing in that drugstore today.

Jimson Weed flower – 3 inches across, belongs to nightshade family from which several pharmaceutical drugs are derived. Used by shamans to induce visions, but misused can kill.

The pharmacy in the back of the store had shelves of ingredients, jars of mysterious ointments along with bottles of odd-sized pills and tablets. Many prescriptions were ingredients compounded by the pharmacist instead of the manufactured ones so common today.

It was there I learned to read doctors' abbreviated dosage orders, and sometimes I was even allowed to count out pills and write instructions for prescriptions, all to be checked by the pharmacist before handing over to the customer.

Soda fountains were a regular fixture of drugstores of this era and I could treat myself to ice cream sundaes and cherry cokes. It was my habit when I arrived after school to make myself a chocolate malt so thick I had to eat it with a spoon. Two inches of walnuts filled the bottom of the malt glass. There must have been a thousand calories in that drink.

I was very thin in those days and this daily dose of sugar, cream and nuts was prescribed by the druggist to "fatten me up." It never did its job, I was naturally lean.

Packaged products like toothpaste, lotions, headache remedies, perfumes and small gifts filled shelves across the room from the soda fountain. I especially remember selling Coty's face powder in round boxes. The design on the box indicated the color and scent of the powder within. And blue-bottled Evening in Paris perfume was a best seller.

At Christmas and for holidays, I arranged gift items to make them appealing in the glass-fronted display cases. It's been a long time since I've thought about my after-school job at the drugstore. I can thank the desert creosote bush for triggering a pleasant memory from my past.

It seems appropriate that the creosote bush should smell like a drugstore since it has long been a source of herbal remedies. Sometimes called the "Indian Medicine Chest," native people used parts of the plant as antiseptics and to heal wounds. A tea made from the leaves was taken to aid in curing an upset stomach, colds, tuberculosis and even venereal disease. Bathing in the tea was thought to ease rheumatism.

Just recently, a botanist friend of mine advised me to make a paste of the leaves to apply on scratches and small cuts. "No other medication is needed and it hastens the healing," she said. I have yet to try it because I tend to ignore small abrasions regularly inflicted on my arms and legs from reaching into prickly bushes and walking through desert brush.

The creosote plant was so useful medicinally, it was recognized and listed in the U.S. Pharmacopoeia from 1842 through 1942 as an expectorant and pulmonary antiseptic. Considering the many uses for remedies in the past, researchers are currently studying creosote to see if it has potential for curing cancer.

In addition to its medicinal value, Native Americans used resin from the bush as a glue for affixing arrowheads and mending pottery. In Mexico today, the flower buds are eaten after pickling in vinegar. And a remarkable chemical from leaves and twigs of the plant is used commercially to prevent or delay oils and fats from turning rancid.

The peanut butter in your refrigerator or pantry may be kept fresh by courtesy of the creosote bush. Even the twigs and leaves, after removal of the resins, provide a livestock feed with as much protein as alfalfa.

It's important to note that the creosote used as a preservative for telephone poles and fence posts is a coal tar product and has no relationship to the creosote bush *(Larrea tridentata).*

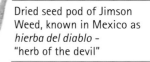

Leaf and fruit of Jimson Weed (Sacred datura) – highly poisonous

It's hard to imagine another plant with so many beneficial uses. Yet creosote bushes are abused and trashed in the desert terrain. Off-road vehicle users routinely drive over their new sprouts and crush their branches.

Developers strip the land clean of them before building. Few homeowners are educated to treasure a creosote bush as a landscape plant. But it is truly a beautiful shrub as well as one that is extremely drought resistant.

February through August the bushes are covered with small yellow flowers, the petals twisted like fan blades. In the summer, when the desert is parched and dry, the clumps of green we see polka-dotting the landscape are creosote, one of the few shrubs able to survive in searing summer sun and through years of little or no rain. The tangy clean smell of the desert after a shower is the creosote bush reminding us of its presence.

Dried seed pod of Jimson Weed, known in Mexico as *hierba del diablo* - "herb of the devil"

As the most abundant shrub in the Sonoran Desert, the bush stands out with an attractive spreading of gray-white branching emanating outward from the base. Darker rings decorate each woody stem in short intervals, and the tiny leaves have a waxy feel from a coating that reduces water evaporation and enables the bush to thrive in the dry desert heat. In a severe drought of several years without rain, the bush may even drop its leaves, but remain alive to put out new ones at the first rain.

One of the things that drew my attention to the bush when I first moved to the desert was a round, brown mass a little smaller than a golf ball fastened to some of its branches. Later I discovered it is a leafy gall caused by a fly, the

small bottles found in desert

Creosote Gall Midge, (*Asphondylia spp.*), and apparently does not harm the bush.

Another amazing aspect of the shrub is its ability to reproduce by cloning. As sprouts are sent up from where the bush germinates, the original plant dies, but its clones grow outward in a circle. If wind is constant from one direction, the clones can only survive on the leeward side of the plant, thus creating a line of bushes instead of a circle.

In the Coachella Valley, one bush is thirty-six feet long. Tests show it to be at least 500 years old. But the "King Clone" creosote with a confirmed age of 11,700 years, exists in the Johnson Valley area of the Mojave Desert to the north. Compare that to known ages of other ancient plants, the bristlecone pine at 5,000 years, a giant sequoia dated from tree rings in its stump at 3,200 years, and Antarctic lichens about four inches across at 10,000 years. That makes the creosote bush the world's oldest living plant.

Sometimes I wish plants came with built in labels - an indestructible tag extolling their special virtues and idiosyncrasies. Would those who look at the desert landscape and say, "There's nothing out there," be more appreciative if they knew the most abundant plant in their view is nature's drugstore of remedies?

Its medicinal qualities alone are enough to make the creosote a valuable desert plant. But in addition, it provides cover and shade for a wide spectrum of wildlife. Pocket mice and other small creatures feast on its seeds, jackrabbits rest under its shady branches, and a multitude of insects live in the leaf mulch at its base. Life in the desert can be precarious and all plants and animals together are needed for their survival and ours as well.

creosote gall

Creosote, the oldest living plant on earth, is not only a model of adaptation and survival, but also an example of nature's gifts to man. Yet it's virtues are unknown to most people including those who have lived in desert areas for many years.

Articles appear periodically to warn the public about the perils of ingesting a tea made from Sacred Datura or Jimson Weed. Well-known by Native Americans as a vision-inducing drug, today's teenagers sometimes attempt to experiment with the plant. Numerous deaths have occurred during this dangerous process.

So while warnings are publicized about Jimson Weed, we never hear of the benefits of the creosote bush. More of the population is informed about endangered species than this most common and abundant desert shrub.

I am hopeful that, as residents become knowledgeable about the outstanding characteristics of this indigenous bush, they will recognize its true value and respect its place in the wild as well as in our yards and gardens.

The next time it rains and the fresh, herbal smell of wet desert permeates the valley, think of the remarkable creosote bush and appreciate the clean scent it lends to the desert air.

As the morning sun continues to warm the land and my walk is nearly over, I pick a few sprigs of creosote and tuck them into my hiking pack. I've acquired some new bleeding scratches on my legs and I think this time I will make use of the desert drugstore.

"Lots of people talk to animals. Not very many listen, though. That's the problem."

- Benjamin Hoff, The Tao of Pooh

Owls and Hecklers

After a leisurely walk down a sand-paved wash and over wind-driven dunes covered with creosote bushes, I arrive home hungry and ready for breakfast. With the morning sun laying its soothing warmth across my shoulders, I settle down in the grape arbor to eat my bowl of oatmeal and read the paper.

Without warning, a loud ruckus erupts in the tall eucalyptus trees framing the north side of my backyard. The caws and shrieks remind me of the noise from a flock of wild parrots that frequented the beach area of my old neighborhood. *There can't be wild parrots here in the desert.* I think, as I leave my bowl of cereal and get up to investigate the raucous screeching.

Standing in the shade of the eucalyptus trees, I can make out a shape, like a football on end, balanced high in the upper branches of a huge old mesquite tree on the edge of the eucalyptus grove. I go into the house for my binoculars and train them on the mysterious lump in the tree. A black hooked beak, devilish-looking tufts resembling ears and two big, round, yellow-ringed eyes stare back at me. It's a Great Horned Owl.

With binoculars focused on the huge bird, I watch as a Cooper's Hawk glides into my view and dive-bombs the owl, swoops upward and plummets back again. After a series of these menacing maneuvers accompanied with shrieking and scolding, the hawk settles on a limb about ten feet away.

Much smaller than the owl, the hawk persists in its heckling behavior. It's beak opens and closes as it emits a continuous sharp *kek, kek, kek.* Had I not seen the hawk land, its spotted rufous breast blending with the leafy shadows of the tree would completely disguise its presence. After a few minutes, the angry hawk finally stops its unsuccessful assault and soars away through the trees leaving the steadfast owl still planted high among the branches.

Fascinated by this newcomer to my yard, I train my binoculars back to the owl, just as a tiny hummingbird flies up near the owl's talons. It hovers, circles the owl and helicopters away. I can't help but think the tiny hummingbird must have been as curious as I but maybe living a little dangerously since a Great Horned Owl's dinner menu of small mammals and rodents also includes small birds.

Even though this owl *(Bubo virginianus)* is common throughout North America, Canada and Mexico, I never anticipated seeing one in the dry desert. Of the six species of owls that have found a way to live in the deserts of the Southwest, the Great Horned Owl, Western Screech Owl, Burrowing Owl, Elf Owl and Ferruginous Pygmy-Owl all belong to the same family, *Strigidae.* Only the Barn Owl, with its white, heart-shaped face is placed in its own family, *Tytonidae.*

Burrowing Owls *(Athene cunicularia)* are the most visible here in the desert because they perch on the ground during the day. Small brownish birds only nine to eleven inches high, they feed on insects and small rodents.

They are almost comic in the way they stand watch outside of their burrows in the ground. I wish the famous cartoonist, Chuck Jones, who gave us roadrunner and coyote had played with the antics of Burrowing Owls, as well. They are cute and I'm sure he could have made them characters we'd all love.

They nest in deserted holes in the ground abandoned by some other desert dweller. Their young have a unique method of protecting themselves from predators. When frightened, the baby owls click their beaks together, much like the way our teeth chatter with fright. The sound is similar to a warning rattle made by a rattlesnake.

Whether this behavior came about by accident or by imitation is unknown. But it's ironic they use a rattlesnake-like sound as their protection, since snakes are also one of the main predators of baby owls.

In the first few months after we moved to the desert, my husband, while forging a walking path around the ranch, discovered a pair of Burrowing Owls living on the side of a hill above our house. Each morning, as he went out to add a few more yards to the trail, both owls would be resting outside their nesting burrow looking like fat little elfins rocking on their front porch. As he approached, they'd fly off to a pile of rocks across the wash and wait until he was gone before returning to their nesting burrow in the side of the hill.

The first time I followed his path, eager to get a look at the owls, our dog, Geronimo, trotted ahead and frightened them away. After several days with the same result, I left Geronimo at home and tried sneaking up on the owls from another angle. Finally I was able to get a good look at these fetching little ground-perching birds.

I really like having the owls nearby as a part of my environment, and just as I had accepted them as regular ranch residents, the unacceptable occurred. There on my front step one morning lay a dead Burrowing Owl in perfect condition except for a small, but deep wound in its neck.

At first I thought Karnak, the outside cat, might be the culprit and had left the offering on my doorstep as a gift, the same way she leaves parts of baby rabbits and rodents. I was annoyed and saddened she'd picked on one of the owls that had taken up residence on the ranch and in my heart.

Later on I found out from a naturalist friend, that it was more likely a hawk was the killer. "Hawks," he said, "grab the owl on the fly, dig in and deliver the death blow to the neck using their razor sharp talons." With both Red-tailed Hawks and Cooper's Hawks in residence I realized Karnak was innocent.

My concern was for the remaining Burrowing Owl. Would it leave the ranch to find a new mate? A few months later I breathed a sign of relief when two owls flew up from their burrow on my husband's walking path.

Burrowing Owls are not endangered and are plentiful in some areas, but I'm glad at least one pair has found a home near my home where I can enjoy their presence.

Catching a glimpse of the Great Horned Owl resting in a tree next to my house during the day is special because I'm unlikely to see the owl during its nocturnal hunting forays. And I never would have looked up into the tree and into the big round eyes that focused back on me if the noisy Cooper's Hawk hadn't alerted me to the daytime hangout of the owl.

The hawk was protecting its territory and wasn't interested in sharing its food source of rabbits and small rodents with a huge owl. Although, since I've seen several varieties of hawks in the tall trees shading my yard, the hawks are sharing my yard whether they are happy about it or not.

I also find owl pellets at the base of a tall palm tree with a skirt reaching almost to the ground. Owl pellets are the undigested regurgitated fur and bones of an owl's meal. One pellet, I took apart contained the entire skeleton of a small rodent with the skull intact.

The pellets are huge, some two inches long, so I know they're from a big bird. Great Horned Owls are big, from fifteen to twenty-five inches tall. From the ground below it's hard to estimate size, but I'm guessing the owl in my mesquite tree is probably a young one in the eighteen-inch range.

Several hours after the first viewing of the owl, it remains in the same place in the tree. Round yellow eyes follow me as I shift to different spots beneath the leaf canopy for a better view through the branches.

The owl, very aware of my presence, watches me as I watch it. At last, since I have other things to do, I go back into the house.

Several hours later, more hoarse cawing brings me outdoors once again to the owl in the tree. A flock of ravens has appeared. They circle and make close darting passes at the owl. It's as if reinforcements have arrived and a concerted effort is being made to get rid of the intruding owl.

I try to count the ravens, but they circle so erratically, cawing and swooping, I can only estimate their number at about twenty. The owl swivels its head around to follow their movements. Facing almost backwards, it reminds me of a toy figure with a loose bobble head.

The ravens have the same goal as the Cooper's Hawk. They are unwilling to share their territory with that of another hunter.

Hawk talons

Red-tailed Hawk feather

Coopers Hawk feather

I have never before seen more than two or three ravens at a time, so where did they find the army they brought to intimidate the owl?

The ravens have a reputation for running off other kinds of birds, so I'm not too keen on having them around. However, the choice is not mine. Fortunately their nest is away from my house in another grove of trees, so this part of my yard is not their immediate territory, but their actions today tell me they lay some claim to it anyway. I enjoy having all of the birds around my home; I just wish they could get along together. But I can't change nature's ways.

During the day, I spend as much time as I can keeping watch on the owl. At one time, a pretty olive-yellow Verdin, a tiny desert bird, flits around inside the tree's leafy branches and, like the hummingbird I saw earlier, it seems unconcerned with the owl.

From a gentle sunny-morning beginning, the sky turns sullen. Thunder rumbles in the distance and an occasional loud crack booms through gray overcast as an overhead cloud releases raindrops, a few at a time. They leave small, damp circles on the concrete patio.

But the promise of rain merely teases, and soon golden rays of sunshine slant through the branches of the mesquite tree.

Several hours after their first attack, the raven gang returns and continues to heckle. I keep wondering if the owl will be annoyed enough to fly away. I want it to stay, but I would also be interested in observing its flight pattern.

Owls are silent fliers. Their soft feathers are arranged so they make no sound as they move through the air. It's the acute hearing of owls that helps them locate their prey by the slightest sound, but the prey cannot hear the noiseless flight of an owl on the hunt.

After nearly half an hour of constant cawing, the ravens again fly off. The owl remains. All day the Great Horned Owl has claimed its perch on the uppermost limb of the mesquite tree.

I continue checking and find it still there as daylight dims and dusk descends. Feeding time for nocturnal hunters has arrived, and the next time I look out in the twilight of early evening the owl is gone.

Some might think spending time watching an owl sit in a tree is time wasted. For me it was time well spent. My understanding of my own life is enhanced when I have the privilege of observing the behavior of wild creatures who must fend for themselves.

Their habits stem from residual genes evolved through centuries. While I, too, have residual genes, I am also backed up with the rules of an organized society, a whole civilization and a choice of religious tenets.

I don't know the origin of the owl as a symbol of wisdom throughout the centuries and in many societies. But I do know I have learned some wisdom from the owl in my tree today. It refused to be driven away. When It finally left, it was on its own terms.

I saw quiet steadfast determination winning out over noisy heckling. With this simple example to guide me, I have no excuse for not behaving as wisely and compassionately as possible within my own learned experiences.

"My understanding of my own life is enhanced when I have the privilege of observing the behavior of wild creatures."

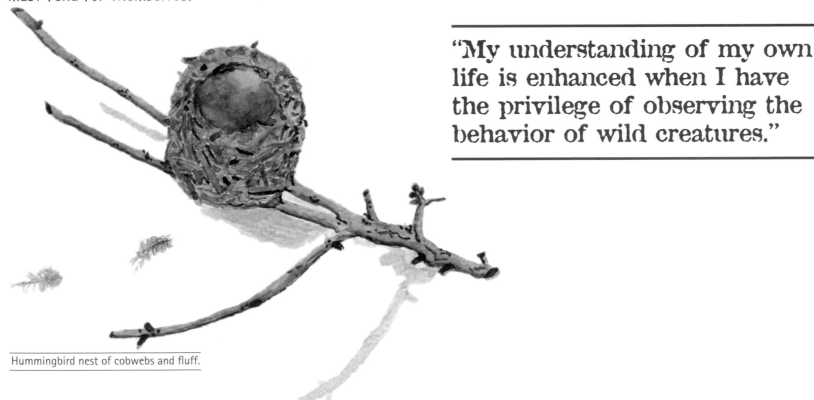

Hummingbird nest of cobwebs and fluff.

"We cannot direct the wind, but we can adjust the sails."

- Unknown

Wind Weather

I awaken to another morning of clear blue skies and mild shirt-sleeve temperatures, a perfect day for some outside maintenance work. I sit down to my breakfast as a soft breeze begins to fan the patio. It feels fresh on my skin and gently rustles the palm fronds around the koi ponds.

By the time I finish my second cup of coffee, the soothing morning breeze has become a wind that whips through tree tops and propels leaves along the ground like toy race cars on an off road competition. The palm fronds no longer sway, but instead, battle against each other with a sound that makes me think of chattering teeth.

I realize every day can't be idyllic, so I decide to go ahead with my plan to work with Manuel, one of our ranch hands to clean up the debris and trash that accumulates around the outside of our entrance gate. Bubbling Wells Ranch doesn't have horses or cows, just trees, so we rake and prune rather than curry and brand.

Since the acreage adjacent to our land is mostly open desert, our perimeter fences catch wind-carried debris like fish in a net. People don't realize a dropped candy wrapper, plastic bag or sheet of Styrofoam can be picked up by a gust of wind and carried for miles before it's caught in a bush or against a wall.

In greener climates with lots of undergrowth and tall grass, small debris is hidden in the foliage and anything organic decomposes during the winter. But here in the desert, every tiny bit of foreign matter sticks out like a beacon on the bare sand. So periodically we spend a day cleaning up other people's trash that has blown onto our property.

Some of the worst offenders are plastic bags. They get caught on prickly pear cactus and Teddy bear chollas and lodge in the limbs of creosote bushes. On a trip to the Sahara Desert in Tunisia, where they also have winds and trash disposal systems are almost none existent, our guide said they call the bags littering the landscape "desert roses." But I think it's far too nice a name for the ugliness created by scattered trash.

My plan for today is to clear away some of the small items while Manuel loads the pickup truck with big sheets of splintered plywood blown against our fence from a nearby construction project. Dry fronds shed from tall date palms and clumps of dried up plants already line the truck bed. While Manuel drives the short distance to unload into the dumpster, I begin raking, a job I usually enjoy.

But as I work, gusts of wind scatter my accumulated piles of dry leaves, whip at my shirt, and push my visor askew on my forehead. I try to ignore the wind and continue to pull organic debris mixed with plastic cups and miscellaneous papers from under the lower branches of a large Texas ranger bush.

I reach carefully into a particularly expansive clump of night blooming cereus to collect soda straws, takeout cups and paper. This cactus clump is one of my favorites, but it's especially good at trapping blowing debris.

When the cereus is in flower, exquisite white blossoms four to five inches across pop out on the sides of the pole-shaped, spine-covered stem. The sun's heat during

Cactus Wren,
7 – 8 inches
Largest American wren –
builds nest in spiny cholla clump

the day causes the flowers to close and finally drop off, but new ones take their place until the blooming period is over.

Other types of cactus, agaves, acacia trees, bougainvilleas and Mexican Bird of Paradise bushes thrive on both sides of our wrought iron entrance gate. They all need occasional grooming to look their best. I actually enjoy this kind of work because I find it peaceful and satisfying to see immediate improvement. But today it isn't satisfying nor fun.

The wind which began as a welcome wisp cooling the morning is now a raging monster. It pulls and tugs at my shirt and shorts. Sand whipping through the air stings my bare legs, and worst of all is the noise. It grates on my nerves. I feel raw and irritated.

Gone is the serene, quiet desert I love so much. I'm perfectly aware these screaming winds are a phenomenon generated mostly in the spring and fall when major climate changes are taking place, but I could do without them.

Even as these seasonal winds rage across the desert sands, kicking up dust particles until visibility is reduced to a matter of yards, I know the conditions are temporary and not like sandstorms that occur in deserts around the world.

The *haboob* in Egypt moves on a ten-to-twenty-mile front at thirty miles an hour. A *khamsin* which means "fifty," is thought to last fifty days or fifty hours and a *sirocco* is a hot, dry wind loaded with dust. It can hide the sun as effectively as a heavy overcast. It has an odor and may cause a toxic effect on humans. The Foreign Legion blames it for suicides. At the

least, it brings about depression in women, children and even animals. Mid-eastern men, however, have developed a unique way of handling it. They sleep through it.

Around the world prevailing winds sweep deserts and move soil. When sandstorms occur, it is usually because the wind comes from a different direction than usual. These dust-carrying winds are the ones personalized with names because they are so violent and destructive. I can be thankful that here in the Colorado Desert, we don't have regular sandstorms so destructive we give them names.

Our prevailing winds come from the west, the coastal part of California. Those that blow from the east towards the coast, we have named Santa Anas. They can be strong, but are not known for creating dust storms. Our desert winds may be mean and brutal, but they are also erratic. Thankfully, the extreme windy conditions that create sandstorms are not regular events, but only occur occasionally. Changeability is one of the blessings of the Coachella Valley.

What we do have are days when wind blows through the pass between Mt. San Gorgonio and San Jacinto and strews fine loose sand onto major streets causing traffic backups and road closures. I will soon have to replace the glass in my car windshield because of the pitting caused by driving during some of these episodes. One time the visibility was reduced to a few yards. It was like driving in a sleet storm except for the brown color of the particles.

I never understood the psychological and physiological

Koi

effect of these winds until today. I think back to the urban area I moved from and remember how often neighborhood noise intruded upon my day. A cacophony of sounds from screeching tires and revving engines to clinking garbage cans, lawn mowers and construction hammerings tore at me, shredding the peacefulness of my being.

My desert home is an oasis from those sounds, but not today as the noise of the gusting wind is so strong, it seems solid, like a thing I can touch, a wall separating me from the usual quiet of the desert.

It becomes increasingly apparent Manuel can't finish the clean up job. One section of old plywood in his hands nearly takes him off the ground as a strong gust catches beneath it and hefts it airborne. All around us, twigs and small branches sail about like pickup sticks. The tops of tall mesquite trees sway like seaweed waving back and forth in the ocean surge.

It's impossible to continue working outside with the wind constantly tearing at me. I want to scream, *Stop, stop blowing things around, stop the noise, stop touching me.*

This is not the first time I have to abandon my plans due to weather and it won't be the last. Nothing I do will change the morning so I must, instead, change what I am doing.

Returning to the house on the golf cart, gusts of gritty air buffet me and rock my light vehicle. They sting the side of my face and drive grit into my nostrils and ears. I close my eyes leaving only a narrow slit in an effort to keep out the blowing particles. All I can think of is the sanctuary of the house and standing under a shower of cleansing water.

Another day, one that is pleasant, will be adequate for finishing today's job. Accepting the weather and working around its eccentricities is a fact of life. Without changes and unforeseen extremes, the world might be a paradise, but bland. Change stimulates and excites. It is the salt and pepper seasoning of life sprinkled on each day's plate of nourishment.

"In the end our society will be defined not only by what we create but by what we refuse to destroy."

- John Sawhill

Painted Ladies

Small winged insects fly at my car, splash against the windshield, and hurl across the road in crazy patterns. The air is thick with flying bugs and I feel as if I'm driving through a storm of black snow. The air stream created by the car's movement carries some of their nearly weightless bodies around and over the hood of the car. *What is this swarm of bugs?* I think.

Painted Lady – feeds on thistles and mallows.

I have heard about locusts and grasshoppers and cicadas appearing in huge numbers, but I'm not aware of any unusual infestation of insects in the area, so what is going on? Just then a ray of reflected sunshine crosses my view like a spotlight and illuminates a sea of orange and black wings. Then I remember reading in the morning newspaper the Painted Lady butterflies have arrived.

The next morning, as I take my walk along the curving shoreline of a small man-made lake, a tree on the south shore has a strange look about it. From a distance I can't discern anything specific, just that it looks different.

I continue on through knee-high grass growing lush along the water's edge until I reach the tree. It is a carob in full bloom and covered with Painted Lady butterflies flitting, perching and milling around. They hang en masse on the sweet-scented blossoms like living ornaments on a Christmas tree. Two very happy roadrunners scurry around its trunk grabbing butterflies out of the air and snatching up any on the ground.

When I take out my digital camera to document the scene, with butterflies dipping and swirling from flower to flower to tree trunk, all I get is a picture speckled with unidentifiable black dots. I select an individual and stalk it, trying to keep it in the camera's viewfinder so I can zoom in and take a close up shot, but as soon as I am ready to snap the picture, the butterfly flits away.

I continue trying to capture a butterfly on film, but they simply won't cooperate. I think maybe I'll do better photographing one resting on a white Desert Chicory flower growing at the base of the carob tree. But before I can click the shutter, the Painted Lady flutters off to another flower head where it alights for a brief moment before taking off into the breeze. I try unsuccessfully to zoom in on butterfly after butterfly, but each one darts away a second too soon. Finally I give up and decide this is one of those events I must record in my memory bank since I can't capture it with a picture.

The onslaught of butterflies intrigues me and I spend some time researching their origins. Looking a lot like small Monarch butterflies, Painted Ladies arrive seasonally in the desert. In drier times, their numbers are small, but in extra wet years with exceptional wild flower displays, their larvae have lots of food and an abundance of Painted Ladies emerges.

As I remember from grade school, butterflies begin as eggs, hatch into caterpillars, then go into a chrysalis stage from which through a process called metamorphosis they emerge transformed into the lovely, elusive creatures we know as butterflies.

I especially like the way young Painted Lady caterpillars, greenish with black spots and bristly hairs, protect themselves while feeding. They bring edges of a leaf together and tie it around themselves with silk from their mouths. The leaf forms a protective casing and allows the larva to munch away in its own little hidden haven. As it grows, it finds a larger leaf and then another until the last leaf becomes a part of its chrysalis.

When the butterflies emerge from the chrysalis, they begin their flight north. Unlike Monarchs that migrate south to Mexico where they were born, Painted Ladies emigrate north and travel hundreds of miles before they

Measuring worm Looper moths – largest family in the order *Lepidoptera* with 2,700 N. American species

die, never returning to their birthplace.

We are aware of two main flyways for their emigration, one up the eastern or desert side of the San Jacinto and Santa Rosa mountains into the Sierra Nevada and beyond, the other up through Arizona and Utah into the Rocky Mountains. We don't know why they almost always fly north. In good butterfly years, millions of these delicate creatures make this long trip only to die at the end of their flight.

I'm glad we don't know everything about these lovely creatures that draw our attention and delight us when they appear in our gardens and yards. A little mystery adds to their allure. It took a spectacular wildflower year in the desert to provide the ideal conditions for the hatching of hordes of these butterflies. This year's multitude has been equaled in only four other years since 1958 and most likely will be the largest I will ever see.

In my experience, I have never before encountered swarms of any kind of butterflies. I only knew it was possible because of the Monarch butterfly migration publicized in recent years, and I assumed it was unique to Monarchs.

More familiar to me are accounts of locusts with their reputation for appearing suddenly in numbers so horrific as to cover the ground and devour every green plant in their path. The havoc caused by plagues of these insects is well known and recorded as far back as in Biblical times.

In this century, killer bees slowly advancing north, merge with local hives and present a bee peril never before experienced. Grasshoppers are notorious for crossing the land in masses while eating everything they perch on, and thousands of cicadas emerging all at once from their underground phase can fill the air with bugs. But never had it occurred to me butterflies might invade in numbers too large to comprehend, much less count. Painted Ladies changed all that when they appeared this spring.

Every so often some element of the natural world explodes and changes the balance of living creatures. A temporary abundance of one species of insect is a common example. The cause and effect of these imbalances are unpredictable.

Monarch butterflies, famous for their migration journey of over 2,000 miles from the eastern United States and Canada to the central state of Michoacan in Mexico, suffered an estimated kill of 500 million one year due to an unexpected freeze. With a drought the following year, it was thought the butterflies would be much diminished. Instead, from 200 to 500 million showed up, reminding us of how little we know of nature's capricious ways.

One thing we do know is the biggest threat to butterflies is man, not nature. The explosion of butterfly populations occurs because their host plants, those they feed on, are plentiful. Throughout the world, an estimated 44% of high quality forests where butterflies hibernate has been degraded.

Butterflies, like other wild things, do not recognize political boundaries, so measures to preserve them need to be worldwide. Just as they go through metamorphosis, changing from egg to larva to chrysalis to butterfly, I think we need to change our ways of thinking about nature one step at a time. We need to figure out how to allow it to exist in and around our world of creeping urbanism.

In this year of Painted Lady abundance, butterflies continue to appear daily in massive numbers. As the daylight of spring lengthens a fraction each day on its way towards summer, the influx of Painted Ladies diminishes. I can't help but wonder what infinitesimal particle of DNA within each tiny body points it northward, and if it senses that death awaits at the end of the arduous journey.

I won't miss driving through hordes of butterflies decorating my car with bits and pieces of their flattened remains, but I will miss seeing them on my walks. Something about the way they flutter around, up, down, sideways, over, about, gives me a feeling of carefree levity.

They take away the weightiness that gravity attaches to my body. To me the butterflies represent a gentler part of nature - beauty and happiness and freedom.

Mysteries abound in this desert, a land of surprises. Instead of the rattlesnakes I expected, I experience flocks of butterflies. I've learned a lesson about preconceived ideas. Isolated bits and pieces of information do not describe a land. Only time can draw the real picture of a place.

White-lined Spinx, heavy bodied -feeds on flowers

"In the short period I have lived in the desert, I've discovered exotic extremes and unexpected delights. I can hardly wait to see what comes next."

"That which we elect to surround ourselves with becomes the museum of our soul and archive of our experiences."

- Thomas Jefferson

On Shaken Ground

As I take my morning walk and gaze at the massive mountain dominating my view, it is hard for me to believe it grows taller by an average of fifteen inches a year, which makes Mt. San Jacinto the fastest growing mountain in the world, surpassing the mere seven-inch rise of the stately Himalayas.

Born eons ago of white hot magma, the mountain continues to thrust upward. At times, birthing spasms shake the rock and rumble along fissures underground. Granite crumbles, boulders tumble as the mountain pushes upward through earth's crust. When all is quiet, and the struggle to escape its molten lava womb subsides, the stately peak of San Jacinto, soars skyward another increment. And so the process of mountain building continues.

But during the process of growing taller, other cataclysmic forces work to tear it down. Snow gathers on San Jacinto's peaks, freezes in cracks and crevices and splits rocks into smaller pieces. Fierce winds erode granite outcroppings and during infrequent thunderstorms, rain pounds the ground washing silt and shattered stone into canyons below. Melt water carries away minute granules and storms shear off projecting surfaces. So over a year's time, as much of the mountain is worn away as is built up.

Mt. San Jacinto at 10, 834 feet remains a little sister to its twin, 11,485 foot Mt. San Gorgonio, the tallest mountain in southern California. Together the two peaks frame the west entrance to the Coachella Valley.

Anyone driving east on Interstate 10 follows an historic trail through the pass between Mt. San Jacinto and the Santa Rosa Range on the south and towering Mt. San Gorgonio on the north, a part of the San Bernardino Mountain chain. In between lies the great Coachella Valley desert, known as the Sonoran or Colorado Desert, which blankets the southwest corner of California and extends into New Mexico, Arizona, Utah and Nevada.

We who live in the Coachella Valley and look up at the peaks and mountain ranges surrounding us often take the beauty and majesty of our valley for granted. When I am out walking my favorite desert paths in the early morning, I never cease to marvel at the shifting moods of the mountains.

Towering over the valley, purple shadows fade as the sun rises, pink ice cream topped-peaks blend into hazy shapes as the first rays of dawn cast their glow across the landscape. A sprinkling of snow in winter on the highest peaks grows to a whipped cream swirl that lasts until late spring. Clouds drift across steep slopes and sometimes obscure most of the mountain.

Some days, all I can think of as I gaze at the grayish behemoth, is old velvet, worn and threadbare in places, but still inky black in shadowed ravines. Subtly shifting hues form new patterns as I watch. Just like ocean waves, mountain scenery is never static, but transforms hour by hour as it unveils an altered face to the valley below.

For those of us who live in this elongated basin rimmed with stately mountain peaks, it is natural to take this extraordinary beauty for granted. Few of us think about how the desert landscape came about or how it breathes and builds new land. We forget the Sonoran Desert only exists because two continental plates collide and in the process push up mountains.

This area of the Sonoran Desert is geologically active and while we tend to think of the ground under our feet as stable, sometimes it isn't. Small earthquakes are common, but always disconcerting. Having chosen to live here for other reasons, we go along daily pushing fear to the back of our closet of anxieties as we find other stresses to fill up our days. Then we are surprised when solid ground pitches and rolls as sliding continental plates adjust to new positions.

Thoughts of massive, destructive earthquakes do not come easily in the quiet, relaxed desert surroundings. But the possibility of a devastating quake looms ominously in the dark recesses of my mind.

One segment of the seven hundred fifty mile long San Andreas fault cuts a swath across our property. Not so apparent on ground level, but easy to see from the air, the fault line is a narrow band of green in an otherwise dry landscape. Available ground water where the fault cuts into earth's crust, nourishes plant growth.

Credit must also be given to earthquake faults for palm oases sprouting unexpectedly in otherwise dusty, rock canyons. Where water rises close to the surface through a crack in the earth, it feeds the roots of thirsty trees. Waterfalls and streams in mountain fissures always surprise me when hiking through dry terrain.

The Indian Canyons in Palm Springs have running water year round and supported a substantial population of Native Americans long before any white man set foot on desert land. Hot springs from thermal underground sources were used by early people just as they are a popular attraction today

One day on my way to a conference a few miles away in Palm Springs, a 5.4 earthquake shook the nearby mountains and desert floor. In my car, I didn't feel a thing, but when I

arrived at the hotel site, everyone was excitedly describing their reaction to the quake.

For many of the out-of-state visitors, it was their first earthquake experience. Their stories varied depending upon how many floors up their rooms were located. I listened with mild amusement and a faintly jaded attitude having felt numerous quakes during my years living in California.

However, earthquakes are no laughing matter and even minor ones can cause death and destruction. In the 1992 – 7.3 magnitude Landers quake, the only human casualty was a baby whose crib was hit by bricks falling off a fireplace. That one death was a tragic occurrence.

Earthquakes are not solely a desert phenomenon. All of the land west of the Rockies is still building due to the movements of continental plates. There are large active fault lines and smaller offshoots. A fault line map placed over the Coachella Valley looks as if an irregular cobweb has been placed on top of its topography.

We are told the big one will hit sometime in the valley and is long overdue. The small shakers and rumbling we receive every so often are but reminders the peril is real and could strike at any time.

The first major quake I experienced took place in 1971 while we were living in Los Angeles.

When the 6.6 Sylmar temblor hit, my husband and I jumped out of bed to rush up the hallway to the children's rooms. The house swayed so much it was all we could do to stay upright with our arms extended out sideways to the hallway walls.

When it was over, the children were fine, the youngest had slept through it. A picture had fallen off the wall, the swimming pool water still sloshed back and forth like a tidal wave, but there was no damage. The pier and beam construction of our house allowed it to rock and sway without harm.

Elsewhere, over thirty people died in a collapsed building, freeway exchanges fell leaving huge yawning gaps in the pavement and homes were jiggled off their concrete foundations. There is no avoidance of earthquakes and the best anyone can do is be prepared with a survival plan.

Now, years later in a different location, I look out at Mt. San Jacinto standing tall and overwhelming in its beauty precisely as a result of fault lines and earthquakes. As the Pacific plate subducts beneath the North American Plate, it wrinkles the earth and as a result San Jacinto and the Santa Rosa mountain range are squeezed upward with each new earth movement.

Without the clash of these two major tectonic plates, southern California would be as flat as Kansas, and then we might have to prepare for tornadoes. One of the prices we pay for extraordinarily varied and beautiful landscapes is to live with the constant threat of earthquakes.

Every morning I marvel anew at the grandeur of the mountains surrounding the Coachella Valley. The desert floor may be green and speckled with flowers from spring rains or dry as dust and mostly brown during a searingly hot summer, but the mountains put on different clothes every day. As clouds swirl around their peaks, subtle pastel hues travel across their cravasses and canyons. At sunset, they serve as backdrops for colors so dazzling, words cannot describe them.

I try to give names to the muted tones catching my eye as I stop and gaze at the towering peaks, but descriptive words evade me and I get caught in a maze of muted pinks and purples.

Maybe, I think, it's like the Alaskan native people who have a multiple of words for snow, each with a different shade of meaning. I need more descriptive words to accurately portray the subtle variations in desert light.

When I lived in the Midwest and later on the California coast, I never liked the pastel colors of desert paintings. I thought they looked pale and washed out. I was used to vivid greens and earthy browns and paintbox-colored flowers. Not until I moved to the desert did I understand the delicate variety and quality of desert hues. Now I see them as variations on a theme and they tantalize me by defying description. Maybe it's best that I can't accurately describe desert colors and the varying tints of mountain vistas. All of it's mystery and geologic rumblings would be lost in a sea of definitive words.

Instead of absolutes, my mountain view consists of sensory images tinged with awe. I awake each day knowing there are parts of my world that are unknowable. But if I pay attention and experience them with emotional impact instead of descriptive words, they fill my life with wonder and I can be sure that every day will be different, fresh, and indescribable.

Vulture claw

"Until he extends his circle of compassion to include all living things, man will not himself find peace."

- Dr. Albert Schweitzer

Surprise at the Spa

During a sunset walk with my husband along the hilltop of our property, with Geronimo trotting ahead as leader of the pack, we stop at a bench to sit and enjoy the display of celestial colors performing a slow dance in the western sky. Paintbox orange, purple and gold swirl gently over mountain tops as the sun follows its elliptical path over the horizon. The last tinted rays of light turn to mauve, and as we watch, a few puffy pink clouds retain the glow of a fireball sun whirling its way to shine on another part of the planet.

My husband and I decide a soak in the hot mineral water, that comes up from the ground at 105 degrees, would be a perfect end to this day. We change into our bathing suits and head for the lower spa near the swimming lake. Geronimo rides in the back of the golf cart instead of running along behind as a dog should. Soon we are settled in the rock spa, reclining in soft soothing water to rejuvenate our bodies, our souls already renewed by nature's sky painting.

Leaning my head against the rock wall of the spa, I let my legs and arms float free. I am totally relaxed and enjoying my soak in the healing water, when my husband suddenly sits up straight and says, "Look, it's a snake!"

Startled by his words, I snap my head sideways to follow his line of sight to the edge of the spa behind me. A pinkish rope slowly glides across the stones on the outside of the overflow outlet. The snake is less than a foot away, but outside of the spa and still partially hidden by the rock walls. I spring up out of the hot water and splash awkwardly to the opposite side next to my husband, but curiosity keeps me standing so I can get a better look. I watch with dark fascination as the four-foot-long rosy-colored snake flows over rocks adjacent to the spa, across a patch of sand, past an oleander bush, and finally under a deck next to the pond.

"It's a coachwhip," I say, as I settle back into the hot mineral water. "The sound and vibration of water cascading over the spa spillway must have masked our being here or it never would have come so close and moved so leisurely. My husband, often a skeptic, wants to know how I can tell, since he hasn't seen this type of snake before. I explain that the coachwhip stands out in my mind because it is the only snake in my desert identification books with four separate pictures, each a different color combination, ranging from pink, gray, tan, reddish brown, to black, with tan or black hatch marks.

The coachwhip we just saw was rosy-pink with tan hatch lines and three black rings near its head. A really beautiful snake, if you are one of the people who can call snakes beautiful. I'm quite proud of myself for remembering the pictures in the book well enough to make a positive identification. All those hours paging through guides to the desert finally pays off.

Coachwhips feed on grasshoppers, cicadas, lizards, small rodents and other small snakes and, while this snake is not poisonous, I have read it will bite if handled and can be aggressive with hissing and striking if threatened. None of which is a problem for me, since I have absolutely no thoughts of ever again getting close enough to so much as breathe the same air.

Another name for the coachwhip, *(Masticophis flagellum)*, is red racer, which is quite appropriate since it may be the fastest snake known, with a top speed of three and one-half miles per hour. At thirty-six inches to over eight feet in length and slender as a finger, if I ever saw one in black, I would certainly understand the derivation of its common name, coachwhip. In fact, it is the hatch marks across its body that resemble a woven whip.

Even if you don't like snakes, which I don't, the coachwhip is worth seeing. I can appreciate the beauty of snake color combinations, because it's not the coloration of snakes I dislike, it's their sinuous bodies and the "snaky" way they move that repulses me. I've come to the point of being able to look at a snake and appreciate its beauty, but if it slithers rapidly about, something primitive inside of me is triggered and I have an irrational response, a mixture of fear and revulsion.

If I give in to it, my stomach turns and I feel sick, so I always fight it and try to be rational.

While ranch hands were digging an irrigation trench last summer, the burrow of a Glossy Snake was accidentally disturbed. One of them brought the snake into the house to show me. I was sitting at my desk, and you can imagine my horror when I looked up and standing a few feet away is a person with a writhing four-foot-long snake in his hands.

Fortunately, he had a firm grip on it and the snake actually seemed friendly, no quick darting or striking movements. It appeared to be gently exploring. I was startled, but kept my cool and pulled out the *Audubon Deserts* book to see if I could identify it. I was able to determine fairly quickly that it was a harmless glossy snake *(Arizona elegans)*, another desert denizen entirely new to me.

One of my grandsons was visiting at the time and he wanted to hold it. I was able to take several pictures with it draped around his shoulders. It appeared unintimidating so I got really brave and managed to gingerly place one finger on its shiny cream-colored scales. They felt like smooth plastic.

My grandson was thrilled to hold the snake, I was thrilled to leave it in his hands and not in mine. I got to thinking about how young boys always seem to like snakes and little girls seem to fear them. I know this is not universally true, but it is the pattern. *Why?* I wonder. *Is it because boys have to contain their fear and dislike to confirm their manhood, or are they just naturally less bothered by the "snaky" shape?*

Years ago, on a trip to Singapore, my husband and I were at a festival where a turbaned male carried around a fat six-foot python for pictures with tourists. I watched as person after person posed for a photograph with the huge snake wrapped around their shoulders. Fascinated and repulsed at the same time, I knew it would help me if I could summon up enough courage to have that snake hanging around my neck

Subspecies
of Western
Shovelnose –
10 to 17 inches,
"swims"
through
loose sand.

for the few seconds it would take to snap a picture.

Finally, I was ready. Swallowing my fear and distaste, I said, "I'll do it if you can keep the head pointed away from my face." The snake handler smiled and placed the heavy python on my shoulders distracting it enough so its head faced away from me. My husband took an eternity to focus the camera and at last clicked the shutter. I exhaled, after realizing I had been holding my breath for the entire episode. As the python was lifted from my shoulders, I realized the short episode had taken every bit of my self control.

It was a big step for me to have that snake's skin touching my skin, to feel its weight resting on my shoulders, to sense the contraction of its muscles on the back of my neck as it shifted position. But I had done it and it was over.

I can't wait to show my children this photo, I thought, *they'll never believe it.* At which point my husband said, "Oops, I didn't get the picture. You'll have to do it again."

Our marriage nearly ended right there in Singapore. But then I took a deep breath and thought, *If I could do it once, I can do it again.* The experience certainly didn't make me suddenly love snakes, but it did help me to accept them without an automatic reaction of horror. I now consider them as yet another example of the astounding array of life on planet earth.

That event in Singapore has stayed with me and allows me to watch with interest as the coachwhip meanders through its realm and mine. I know there are other snakes around, some harmless like the coachwhip and glossy, others dangerous like the sidewinder whose tracks I sometimes see in the sand. But snakes stay hidden for their own safety and have no interest in me except as a danger to them. So, when I'm privileged to catch a glimpse of one of these reptiles, I experience a small thrill at seeing the creature in its natural environment. After all, snakes adapted to desert living long before man; I'm an intruder on their territory.

In spite of its harsh climate, the California desert is home to many of the thirty-eight species of snakes found in California. Now that the desert is my home, I need to know with whom I share my environment. Who lives in the sandy burrows I see under creosote bushes and the holes I find hidden in piles of weathered rocks? Who lives beneath brush collected in a ravine? I have much to discover.

My husband and I finally pull ourselves from the luxury of the warm mineral water and head back to the house on the golf cart. This time Geronimo chooses to run behind and get the exercise he needs.

I continue to think about our experience with the coachwhip, and I realize that one of the bonuses of living on wild desert acreage is catching glimpses of true desert dwellers and being reminded of the ways living things adapt to climate.

> "The longer I live in the desert, the more I learn about those creatures who know how to survive extreme heat and dryness. My home would be a sorry place without all of them, who together, give it life and meaning."

"Water is the driving force of all nature"

- Leonardo Da Vinci

Shards from the Past

Day breaks on the desert floor, ushered in with rumbles of thunder and a rare rain always welcome in this dry climate. I delay my walk until midmorning after the skies clear and Thor stills his heavenly hammering.

My goal is to explore an animal trail leading across an earthquake fault that bisects our property. Atop a windswept dune marking the fault line stretching for miles along the northwest side of the Coachella Valley, dense stands of old gnarled mesquite struggle to grow. Their thick and twisted trunks run a constant race to keep their leafy canopies from being swallowed by blow sand that collects around them.

If I had X-ray vision to see underground, I could detect a rent in the earth where one edge of the fault grinds against the other as the Pacific plate of the North American continent moves slowly northward. At the meeting of these plates, the ground is forced upward into a raised scar covered with a green scab of foliage. A shallow water source created by the fault nourishes growth on top of the windblown dune.

As I walk along following rabbit tracks, glistening droplets of moisture cling to the leaves of ancient creosote and mesquite that were growing on this upraised scar when Native Americans were the only humans living in this climate. The air is heavy with the spicy pungent scent of creosote leaves, their distinctive odor enhanced by rain.

A narrow band of rabbit tracks leads me to the edge of a dune. I slide down the steep face of the windblown mound gathering pockets of fine sand in my shoes and socks. I have not walked here before but, since it is regularly used by rabbits and coyotes, I want to see where it leads. Keeping my eye on their prints as a tracker follows a spoor, I hurry along bristling with expectation, my curiosity alerted.

Loose sand on the steep side of the dune causes me to nearly lose my balance, but I regain footing as the ground levels out and a trail veers off towards an area dotted with clumps of saltbush. Alert for any small tidbit of interest, my eyes search the desert floor as I continue on, hoping to come upon something out of the ordinary, something intriguing that captures my attention.

When a small flat rock with reddish tones stands out from other grayish-colored sand granules on the ground, I stoop to pick it up and brush away fine-grained earthen residue clinging to its surface. My heart begins a faster beat, as I realize it is not a rock, but a shard of ancient pottery.

Indians traversed this general area of the Southwest for thousands of years, but my first piece of real evidence confirming their presence is the shard I hold in my hand. Looking around, I see another red-brown-colored fragment lying beneath a clump of golden bush and nearby, with just an edge protruding from the sand, I pick up a third remnant. I kneel and dig with my hands in the soft debris around the base of the bush. Soon I have a mosaic of shards laid out in the fine sand. I count them. Twenty-six pieces of broken red-clay pottery.

Following an animal trail this morning led me to this bed of shards. But long ago it was another person who walked here, another person who carried this pottery vessel across the desert. Perhaps they stopped to camp overnight and the clay pot was used for cooking rabbit stew. Water was available from neighboring Two Bunch Palms where a natural seep of hot water was known to early people. For countless years, palms thriving

Coyote paw prints, claw marks are visible and similar to dogs and wolves

on this underground reservoir marked a water hole for those who understood the desert. With water, mesquite beans and animals for food, this was surely a place many trod before me and found hospitable for desert living.

I fill my pockets with the treasured pottery shards and head for home returning the way I came through the ancient mesquite forest of short bushy trees, some barely reaching above my head. Mesquite beans, a staple food for desert Indians, would have attracted early people to this site and may help explain the remains of the shards I found this morning where they lay abandoned in the sand that hid them for so many years.

Back at the house, I wash the shards in the sink, dry them on paper towels, and lay them on newspaper placed on the kitchen table along with a bottle of white glue. White glue dissolves in water, so it can be used to reconstruct a pot with no harm done to the shards. The glue can always be soaked off, if desired. I select two pieces and move them around to see if they fit next to each other. It takes multiple tries with each piece before I find two edges that mesh. I apply the white glue and hold the pieces together until I think the mend will hold. A tray filled with sand makes a solid, but malleable, bed on which to place the fragments until the glue hardens.

My husband and daughter, both drawn to the process as strongly as I, join me as we work on our pottery puzzle. After hours of fitting and gluing we begin to see the curve of a pot take shape.

With only twenty-six shards, there aren't nearly enough to reconstruct the whole pot, so the next day I go back to the site with high hopes, a brass household strainer to sift through the sand and a beach umbrella to give me shade from the 115 degree heat. I find only five more pieces.

Potsherds have held a distinct fascination for me ever since I had the opportunity to study those with intricately painted designs from the Four Corners area of the Arizona desert. That these remnants of a civilization existing long before mine have remained intact after hundreds, even thousands, of years while lying hidden in pockets and crevices, thrills me with that indefinable sense of excitement treasure hunters know so well. I have to thank the rain for uncovering the first precious relics yesterday. Rain in the desert sometimes does more than water a thirsty land - it may also quench a thirsty soul.

The reddish-brown shards are identified by Harry Quinn, an archaeologist, as typical Tysen brown, normal material for Cahuilla pottery. A few rim pieces indicate the pot opening would have been large, so the remains are most likely that of a cooking pot.

Cahuilla cooking pot made from coiled ropes of clay pounded flat with a paddle

Water jar with small mouth to prevent evaporation and facilitate carrying

Tysen brown clay comes from washes where newly deposited mud curls at its edges as it dries and has a lot of temper in it, so it is heavy and durable. Temper is larger sand granules that help to hold the finer clay material together.

One shard, whitish in color and unlike the others, is buff-ware which came from a water jar and is made from sedimentary clay laid down in layers. It is much finer than Tysen brown. It holds water better by cutting down evaporation through the pottery and functions similar to a canteen.

Evaporation was helpful, however, to early pioneer settlers who used Indian cooking pots to hold water for drinking, since evaporation through the clay cooled the water. In Mexico, this clay water jar *(olla)* tradition continues.

During a trip through the San Francisco Mountains of Baja California Sur to see the giant cave paintings publicized by Earl Stanley Gardner, the mystery writer, I was offered a drink from a Mexican *olla*. Our guide had brought us to a goat farm on our way out of the canyon and, since I had organized the expedition and was the only one who knew a few words in Spanish to communicate, the goat farmer assumed I was the group leader.

Aware we had hiked a long way in the sun and daytime heat, he offered me a drink from his family's clay cup resting on top of their clay *olla*. My first thought was, *I can't drink from the same clay cup this whole family uses daily. When was it last washed?* My second thought was, *It would be extremely impolite to refuse.* So I accepted the family cup with thanks and drank. The water was welcomingly cool. The rest of the group followed suit. Without a word passing among us, we all silently placed acceptance of polite hospitality before worry about hygiene, which wasn't easy since we stood on their *portal* within sight of a skinned and fly-covered slaughtered goat hanging from a beam.

On the table in my kitchen, the piecing together of pottery shards continues, but it does not go quickly. It takes several weeks working in small increments of time while carefully trying all broken edges of one piece against all broken edges of every other piece to find a fit. Unlike a picture puzzle, there are no visual clues. To add to the difficulty, some shards have only a small matching portion instead of the entire edge.

As with most difficult puzzles, we search and search before finding where a piece belongs. Only one shard and one tiny chip does not find a place in the fragmented, glued-together pot section.

Working with these tangible remnants of times past reminds me of a story I read about Native Americans on a Colorado River trip to visit ancient camping sites of their ancestors. The archaeologist guide was baffled by why the Indians didn't seem very excited by the pottery shards and ancestral remains they found at the mouths of canyons. She was disappointed at their lack of interest in any of the artifacts she pointed out. Instead they seemed to be always looking up canyon and acting as if they wanted to go there. After several days of this behavior, she finally succeeded in getting one of the party to explain the problem. The refuse from a lost habitation site is a reminder of the people, but of little importance compared to the reason for the site's existence. The Indians weren't interested in "things" left over from another time; they wanted to see where the water came from to cause their ancestors to camp at these spots. To them, water as a life-giving force was the important element, not left over bits of household refuse. The springs up canyon were alive and sustained life for their ancestors. Once the guide began taking

Tysen brown pottery shards

the group up the canyons to look for water sources and the spirits inhabiting them, everyone was happy.

I find it fascinating to see how cultural differences affect the way people view the world, and I continue to be amazed with the wisdom of Native Americans. They knew what was important and weren't side-tracked the way we are today by all the useless minutia that constantly bombards us.

In the desert, a water source is the reason for living at that site. This is as true today as ever. Without the underground reservoirs in the Coachella Valley, habitation here by hundreds of thousands of people would be impossible. It is still the "spirits" of the springs that sustain us.

While I continue to be fascinated with the pottery shards I was led to by a rabbit trail one damp day after a rain, their message to me is "things" are just "things." They have little intrinsic value. Of course "things" are fun and enjoyable and can serve as potent links to the past, but real values exist in the more essential ingredients for life. It might be a tangible like water, as recognized by Native Americans, or intangibles like love, health, serenity and safety that add quality to life.

When I find myself getting too caught up with my "things, even though they give me great pleasure, I try to remember the Native American way, "revere only that which is alive and provides the reason for living," whatever that may be for my place in time.

"The world is a scene of changes, to be constant
in nature were inconstancy."

- Cowley

Ravenswood

Instead of a desert walk, today I am helping rid the swimming lake of spiny niab, a prickly pond weed we don't want growing where we paddle around enjoying the water on a hot summer day. In the Midwest, our swimming lake would be called a pond, but here in the desert any body of water larger than a swimming pool is labeled a lake. We have the swimming lake, and several others, only because of an underground reservoir of hot water that is here as a result of an earthquake fault that runs through the area.

So here we are, my husband, daughter and two ranch hands, submerged to our thighs, wearing sun hats, working with wooden-handled tools, and looking like rice paddy farmers as we rake the obnoxious weed off the lake bottom. We'll never be able to rid the pond of spiny niab, but our efforts on this quiet, peaceful morning will clear an area along the sandy shoreline large enough to create a pleasant place to enter the water. It will also be nice for my grandchildren to have a weed-free place to play. The first words out of their mouths when they come to visit are, "Can we go swimming?" Which means we spend a lot of time at the swimming lake.

On a Sunday afternoon the six of them will spend hours in the lake. Like kids in the Midwest where I grew up, they take the rowboat out and pull swimmers behind it, crawl in and out, jump off its sides and sooner or later end up tipping it over to play "King of the Mountain," which involves one person balancing on the overturned hull while the others try to make him fall off by rocking and jostling. And always there is

Ravens' egg shells after hatching

ducking underneath into the space of trapped air and echoing voices between water and wood.

I remember from my childhood how spooky it seemed to swim under the upside down boat and come up in that sealed-off chamber of air. Sunlight on the water filtered into the space just enough to give an eerie glow inside the cave-like cavity. Even though I knew everyone else was only a few feet away, I always felt alone under the boat. It was like entering an eerie unknown world. While there was plenty of air to breathe, I could never get comfortable, so I never stayed there more than a few seconds.

The tipped-over boat and all the horseplay along with it are part of the old swimming hole scene. Today's children are better acquainted with backyard tiled pools equipped with a multitude of plastic floats and water toys than they are with natural swimming holes. Swimming pool water is clear and scented with chlorine. Lake water has a mild smell of green-growing plants and the outdoors.

When newcomers arrive at our swimming lake, they are often intimated because they can't see the pond bottom, so they worry about the unknown that might lurk within. They ask about bugs and critters and if anything in the pond will bite them. Even though we assure them there is no danger, they sit on the steps reluctant to enter the dark water until they see everyone else having a good time. Then they forget their fears and join in the old-fashioned fun. It makes me feel good that my grandchildren can come to the "swimming hole" and experience the same kind of imaginative water play I enjoyed in my childhood.

On the southeast shore of the swimming lake a tamarisk grove rises out of a large sand dune. Whether the dune came first or the tamarisk trees, I can't be sure, but I do know the dune builds constantly. By the time the original fast-growing saplings acquired thick trunks and massive branches, so heavy they cracked and fell to the ground with the help of a strong wind, they were growing out of a massive dune.

Now huge fallen tree trunks, at least four feet in diameter, line the edges of the mound, and new growth from each trunk shoots straight upward forming side walls of foliage. Leafy tree tops bend inward and roof over the open center area obscuring it from view.

A gentle breeze fans through thin, elongated leaves hanging like curtains, and a thick carpet of dried needles feels soft and spongy beneath my feet. It soaks up sound, blocking out the world beyond. This inner clearing is always cool so that, on the hottest day, I can walk through an opening in the branches and emerge into a shady green-scented glen.

Filtered sun permeates this enchanted natural arbor, casting a soft glow, a respite from the harsh glare of desert light. I feel like Alice entering the rabbit hole. Unlike the overturned boat chamber, for me this is a comfortable place where dreams come naturally and swirl with kaleidescope visions.

I always have an overwhelming desire to create a nest, a cozy retreat, a playhouse in this secret bower where imagination runs wild. It makes me wonder why the grandchildren haven't been lured into this fantasy domain. I can only guess swimming has captured them so completely, they are content with no need to seek further entertainment.

Yet, the tamarisk grove enchants me. I often stop there when taking my walks. I like to check on the ravens' nest high up in the canopy, and sometimes I find a blue-black feather in the bushes. The ravens prey on small creatures and leave remnants of their last meal on the needle-covered ground. Small puffs of fur and bits of unidentified leavings tell me the ravens are eating well.

At one time I placed a wicker settee with

Raven feather life size 12 inches

puffy cushions in the clearing so I could have a place to sit and enjoy the glade. The ravens tore the cushions apart and used the stuffing for nesting material. I realized then, Ravenswood, as we now call it, is their territory, where they live, and I am only a visitor.

The Common Raven, *(Corvus corax)*, belongs to the order of *Passeriformes* or songbirds which also includes crows, jays and magpies. I would never have guessed ravens, with their raucous croaking, would be in the songbird category. Yet, their strident call seems to fit the harsh desert climate. In the Southwest skies of canyon country, a black raven soaring on unseen thermals, its cry echoing through twisted eroded sandstone walls, is as much a part of the landscape as a coyote singing on a bluff top.

Sometimes mistaken for crows, which do not thrive in the desert, ravens are larger, have a coarser voice and are more versatile. It is the intelligence and adaptability of ravens which enable them to survive in multiple environments from low desert to dense forests and geographically from Alaska to Central America.

They can be predators or scavenge for their food, depending upon availability. They mate for life and have been known to live as long as forty years.

Acrobatic in the way they fly, they swoop, dive and play in the air the way sea otters play in the ocean and my grandchildren play in the swim pond.

Along with parrots, ravens are the smartest of birds. They apply reasoning in situations entirely new to them and are credited with insight behavior at least matching that of a dog. It takes four years for their young to reach adulthood.

A public television program I watched documented ravens figuring out how to steal fish from an untended fishing line. They learned on their own, or perhaps, from watching the fisherman, how to pull the line out of the water in order to get the fish on the hook. On golf courses, they steal and hide golf balls. Who knows what their intelligent bird minds are thinking during this behavior?

Ravens were desert dwellers when early desert inhabitants moved seasonally from the hot desert floor to cooler mountainsides. Their observation of the raven's versatility likely accounts for the many stories about Raven in Native American lore. Raven is smart and tricks Coyote. In Pacific Northwest folklore, Raven uses his trickster skills to steal the sun and bring the gift of light to the people.

Early inhabitants of the desert would have seen ravens, but not in tamarisk trees, since it was not until the advent of railroads that tamarisk was imported to use as windbreaks along train tracks. From those first plantings, tamarisk, also known as salt cedar, sprang up anywhere their wind-carried seeds could set roots and burrow deep into underground reservoirs to gulp water like thirsty behemoths. Now a movement to eradicate tamarisk trees is being implemented throughout the valley.

Since I am environmentally concerned, it may seen strange for me to be so enamored with our glade of these water-guzzling giants. I understand the reason for getting rid of them, but I can't bring myself to cut down Ravenswood. The big old trees forming a tall patch of green in an otherwise sparse desert landscape are simply too beautiful to chop down. For a while at least, I'm keeping my tamarisk grove, with its secret hideaway and ravens nest.

I would, however, love to see the grandchildren give the ravens a little competition with nails and boards and the building of a fort or playhouse in Ravenswood. Or am I, perhaps, too old-fashioned and haven't accepted that today's children play video games instead of building tree houses?

The ravens are, no doubt, relieved there is no pounding and nailing taking place.

As I think about it, since everyone is happy, perhaps it's best for the grandchildren to continue enjoying the lake and leave Ravenswood to the ravens.

By now, the rice paddy workers in the pond are getting sunburned shoulders and need to end weed raking. The rock spa on the edge of the lake is filled with hot water straight from the well and a good soak will be a perfect way to end the morning's work.

Lining the shore are piles of spiny niab left to dry out before being carted away. But I wouldn't be surprised if an enterprising raven searches through them for a snail or other morsel of food. Maybe that's what the one perching atop a tall tree, screeching his annoyance to the wind, is trying to tell us. I would like to remind him, however, he is classified as a songbird and it would be nice if he could adopt a more melodious tone.

Relative sizes of a raven and crow

Common Raven – largest member
of order of *Passeriformes* (songbirds)

Two years later, at the end of August, strong winds whipped through the valley and the big tamarisk trunk carrying the ravens' nest, split and crashed to the ground. Sturdy side limbs like table legs supported the fallen tree trunk and held it several feet above my head. Where the ravens' nest had been, only a few entertwined twigs remained. On the ground below, two blue-black raven feathers rested on a bed of dried tamarisk needles.

"You must collect things for reasons
you don't yet understand."

- David J. Boorstin, Librarian of Congress Emeritus

Collector's Haven

Early morning light slides over the horizon across sand-covered dunes, where it lies trapped under patches of parched vegetation. Elongated shadows slide westward from the base of every bush and slowly shrink as the sun begins its journey across the firmament. Fresh earth-scented air, still cool from the night's low temperature, fills my lungs and lifts my spirit.

As I walk past the small agave nursery my daughter, Holly, has developed on the southern edge of Bubbling Wells Ranch, she calls out to me. "Mom, guess what? I've just found the missing items from my workbench." She had been complaining for some time about how little things kept disappearing from the table where she does her repotting and labeling.

"Look at this," she says, holding out a green plastic pot filled with a strange assortment of items – a leather gardening glove, yellow marking pen, pencil stub, white plastic plant marker, small bits of dried-up cactus, a metal clamp and pieces of twine.

She sets the pot on the workbench and pulls another one from underneath the table. It, too, is stuffed with miscellaneous small things – a scotch tape roll, irrigation parts, dry plant shoots and pieces of green garden tape. As she rummages under the bench pulling out more pots and emptying their contents, the pile of found objects includes a small screwdriver, sections of flex hose tubing, bits of wire, black markers and shiny metal staples.

Holly tells me these are the things that disappeared from her workbench over a period of several weeks. Every day something new was missing and she couldn't figure out who was taking them and for what reason. It never occurred to her it might be a wild creature.

"It appears you have a little packrat friend," I say. We look at each other and laugh.

It was purely by accident, she found the objects stashed in flower pots stacked under her work bench. If she hadn't needed a pot for transplanting a new agave, she would still be baffled by the disappearance of all those small items.

The mystery was compounded by the packrat's use of pots for a nest, since these little collecting critters usually have a burrow or mound as their home. Bits of collected debris around the entrance easily give it away to even the casual observer.

At any rate, the mystery of the missing objects is solved and I leave the shade house to continue my walk. Since packrats are the discovery of the morning, I decide to check on Holly's bead garden as I pass by her house. As an artist, she can't resist adding a whimsical touch to her desert plants. So resting among her exotic cactus specimens are brightly colored baubles and other small treasures.

These trinkets attract a little night visitor who steals some and rearranges others.

Desert Woodrat – eats seeds, bark, yucca pods and spiny cactus.

Most mornings, she finds a few of the beads moved around and several missing. The most vulnerable are shiny blue. They disappear regularly.

One bright orange bead caught in a crack between two stepping stones catches my eye. I remember that yesterday the same bead rested at the base of a small barrel cactus several feet away. I have to assume another packrat is at work in her patio garden.

So far she hasn't found where the missing beads are stashed, and we can't blame the nursery packrat because there were no beads in its collection. Someday we'll probably discover where the stolen booty resides, but until then, it's a mystery we haven't solved. A garden where small treasures are moved around or stolen during the night remains a challenge for another time.

Away from gardens and back in native desert lands, I walk through spindly, dried-up growth on sandy pebble-strewn ground. I look around carefully thinking I might find the packrat's nest.

Desert Woodrat *(Neotoma lepida)*, the name for the species of packrat in my area, makes a den by mounding up sticks, plant debris and pieces of cactus. These nests are often tucked into the base of a thorn-covered cholla and are surrounded by prickly cholla buds. Sometimes the nest is in a pile of rocks or an abandoned ground squirrel burrow. At least two access tunnels are necessary to provide an escape route, should a snake or coyote decide to invade the burrow.

Even though packrats only live a few years, an empty nest is likely to be taken over by another packrat and may remain in continuous use for years. I am reminded of my own use of apartments and homes, all of which were built and lived in by others before me. A few even contained interesting items left by previous occupants.

The most astounding example is my current home, which we bought furnished. It was the choice of the previous owner to simply walk away to begin life anew with only her personal effects. I am still using the supply of wax paper and baggies left in the kitchen drawers.

According to James Cornet, a desert biologist, one packrat nest in the Coachella Valley is over 5,000 years old. As he points out, this nest was begun about the same time the Egyptians were building the first pyramid. I find this amazing. It makes me want to know more about this eight and one-half to fifteen-inch long rodent.

Packrats and other woodrats get all the moisture they need from cactus, seed pods and any available green vegetation. Their caramel-colored urine quickly solidifies and forms an amber-like clump called amberat. These clumps look so much like candy or taffy that starving pioneers crossing Death Valley tried eating them. Not aware of what they were ingesting, one pioneer wrote in a diary, "... it was sweet but sickish and some were troubled later with nausea." Doesn't surprise me a bit.

There are better uses for amberat than eating it. Archaeologists have found it plays an important role in preserving items from the past for study. One packrat nest, protected by both a rock overhang and the arid climate of the Southwest's Four Corners area, has been determined to be as old as 50,000 years. This time period was arrived at using Carbon-14 dating to analyze prehistoric textiles, potsherds and dung of long-extinct animals in the amberat-encased den.

Other debris from the well-preserved nest including plant stems, seeds and leaves, insects, lizard scales and microfossils yielded clues to climate changes over the centuries. Information scientists collected showed how much the Southwest has warmed since the last ice age 11,000 years ago. Where once tropical woodlands flourished, today there are deserts and dry lakes. Who would have guessed these little rodents would provide us with a history of the past stretching so far back before our own generations?

It makes me think of the little thief in Holly's garden shed, collecting treasures for the future. I wonder how he will react when he finds all of his carefully accumulated valuables gone.

In a way, I identify with the packrat because I, also, collect and keep too many things. I don't know why the packrat is a collector, but I assume he has good reasons for his behavior.

I have no excuse for my propensity to save. I blame it on growing up in a frugal family. Living on a farm and in a small town, we saved things because they might come in handy at a later time. We didn't have the shopping options available today, and the garage sale phenomenon had not yet taken over the country. Much like the packrat, with its use of cactus as a safety barrier, we had to use what was available, so it was sensible to save everything in order to have what might be needed at a later time.

I should have grown out of my packrat habit as I got older and didn't have to be so thrifty. Somehow I never made that transition and remain attached to my things. I hate to give up old favorites even when new replacements are so much better.

It doesn't help that I see a use for almost everything. A nicely shaped rock could be a doorstop, a galvanized wash tub would be just the thing for icing down drinks at a barbecue, an esthetically curved branch absolutely has to go in the garden. Living on a ranch in the desert has fed my habit voraciously because of all the room we have to store things.

I do better mentally than physically in clearing out the unnecessary. Somehow, I've grown up with the ability to put outdated ideas and unpleasant experiences behind me. My life has not been hindered by the "keeping" of old wounds from past circumstances. I don't clutter my thoughts with concepts that fill up my brain leaving no room for new ideas. When I think of how refreshing it is to stay mentally uncluttered, I realize it would be equally unburdening to get rid of some of the tangible items filling up my household.

Discovery of the packrat's stolen treasure hoard in the plant nursery potting shed solves one mystery, but more importantly it gives me an insight into my life and my packrat tendencies.

The bead garden night stalker brings to mind another idea to think about – how rich desert life is in rewards when you pay it attention. The key is to notice the small world so easy to miss. An orange bead mysteriously out of place, but easily overlooked holds a story as yet unknown, but intriguing to contemplate.

I continue to learn about myself by observing the wildlife around me. Little vignettes, so easy to miss if my mind were already stuffed with packrat-like collections of thoughts, instead become life lessons carrying me forward. Now my task is to act on what I have learned. I can hardly wait to get home and begin uncluttering my space.

Cactus garden beads

"The ripest thought comes from the mind which is not always on the stretch, but fed at times by a wise passiveness."

- W. Mathews

Bird Ballet

Afternoon

Afternoon summer heat scorches the desert landscape. All small animal life is safely underground, insulated from the sun's cruel heat. Some plants turn their leaves sideways to the sun, leaving only their edges to bear its searing rays. Other plants have simply dried up and are no more than crisp, brown skeletons waiting for lower temperatures and a life-giving rain before bursting out with new growth.

My shorts and sleeveless shirt are dripping with perspiration from transplanting a group of barrel cactus to a better location in my garden. In the dry desert, air temperatures around 100 degrees are still quite tolerable, but today with the thermometer registering 112, and high humidity from tropical storms driven north out of the Gulf of Mexico, working outdoors is a bad idea.

For the past week, thunder echoed over the surrounding mountains, while big white puffy clouds tinged with gunmetal gray threatened rain. One day drops of water actually fell out of the sky for all of ten minutes, but most afternoons, only a few drops squeezed out of stormy clouds to barely wet the ground.

Since I missed my morning walk, an afternoon swim seems like a good way to cool off while providing some exercise as well. It doesn't take long to shed my sweaty clothes and pull on a swimsuit. Grabbing a towel and a cold bottle of water, I head outside to the golf cart, my transportation around the ranch. After driving the electric vehicle lickety-split down the driveway bouncing over pot holes and rough spots in the gravel road, I park near the swimming lake behind a stand of Texas ranger bushes in full purple bloom. Their tiny, gray-green leaves remain on the plant for most of the year but are stiff and brittle, an adaptation to avoid sun damage, and whenever the humidity is high, the bushes burst forth with brilliant deep lavender flowers.

Tossing my towel over a railing, I step down wooden steps to the lake's edge, next to a patch of water lilies in full pink and white bloom. As I slide into the water, a patch of white flashes into my line of sight on the far side of the pond. I look up to see an egret strutting quietly in the shallows, its head pointed downward, while searching for small fish to pluck out of the water. Hardly breathing, I stop and freeze in place. I don't want to frighten away this huge bird, but I am so hot I need to go deeper into the pond or I will simply melt away and disappear in a swirl of

Common Egret *(Casmerodius albus)* 37- 41 inches tall

liquid, like hot fudge melting ice cream.

Moving very slowly, I skim quietly out into the lake with only my head above the surface. The egret raises its head and looks in my direction, but doesn't fly away. I don't swim or splash, but instead hover in place while treading water as my eyes follow the movements of the bird on the opposite shore.

As soon as I am cooled enough to feel comfortable I edge my way back to the wooden steps, gather my towel and water bottle, and stretch out on one of the padded lounges set in a row under a rustic ramada built from four tree trunks with shade cloth stretched over the top for a roof. Out of the sun and cooled by my soak in the pond, I settle down to watch the egret.

As large as a Great Blue Heron (between three and four feet tall) and pure white except for long, black stick-like legs, its true name is Common Egret or American Egret *(Casmerodius albus)*. But there is nothing common about this beautiful creature. With an almost snaky-looking neck terminating in a snowy white head with long pointed beak, the bird steps gracefully along the shallow shoreline, carrying its white body along on dark rod-thin legs. Each slow, calculated step makes barely a ripple on the pond's still surface.

water-bird petroglyph

At first I watch the egret's deliberate movements and the way it concentrates on the water as it fishes. Then I notice how everything on shore is reflected on the glass-smooth surface of the pond. The big old tamarisk grove with its huge trunks and gray-green needle canopy, the palm we don't trim so its skirt of dead fronds will provide a haven for birds, clumps of sagey desert bushes and two white rowboats pulled up on shore are all duplicated, their images repeated on the pond's liquid mirror. Above it all, Mt. San Jacinto thrusts upward in a cloud-filled sky, its reflection pointed in the opposite direction on the still surface of the lake. One white egret, connected with its mirror image, becomes two Siamese twins joined at their feet.

Distant thunder explodes somewhere in the mountains and lighting flashes atop San Jacinto. The clouds reflected in the water turn blue-black. I wait for the storm to hit while I watch the egret continue to stalk tiny pond fish along the shoreline, seemingly unaware of the drama in the sky. I find myself mesmerized by the real egret and its twin in the water as the two perform a perfectly synchronized dance - a slow, sensual ballet. Each minor gesture of the egret, mimicked perfectly by its reflection, creates a new picture similar to the one before yet slightly different. A turn of head, tilt of body, coil of neck, every movement performed by two birds, the real and the reflection. Like a kaleidoscope, the slightest change in posture creates a different pattern. Upright standing image and upside down image, twins connected by two black wire legs. The egret ceases being a bird and becomes, instead, a motif, a design evolving gracefully from one variation to another, never repeating the same pattern.

I stay at the pond, intent to enjoy theater in the wild, a bird ballet accompanied by a symphony of thunder punctuated with flashes of stage lightning. Finally the curtains are pulled on the last bit of blue sky and the world above turns gray with moisture. A few tiny droplets escape the clouds and polka dot the sand around my chair. The egret's crisp image reflected in the water blurs for a moment as the glassy surface wavers, disturbed by a few drops of rain.

Then all is still again. The egret continues its graceful dance of existence. The bird across the pond has its place, I have mine, and the beauty of it is we are both here by choice - the egret finding food for its body, I feasting on nourishment for my soul.

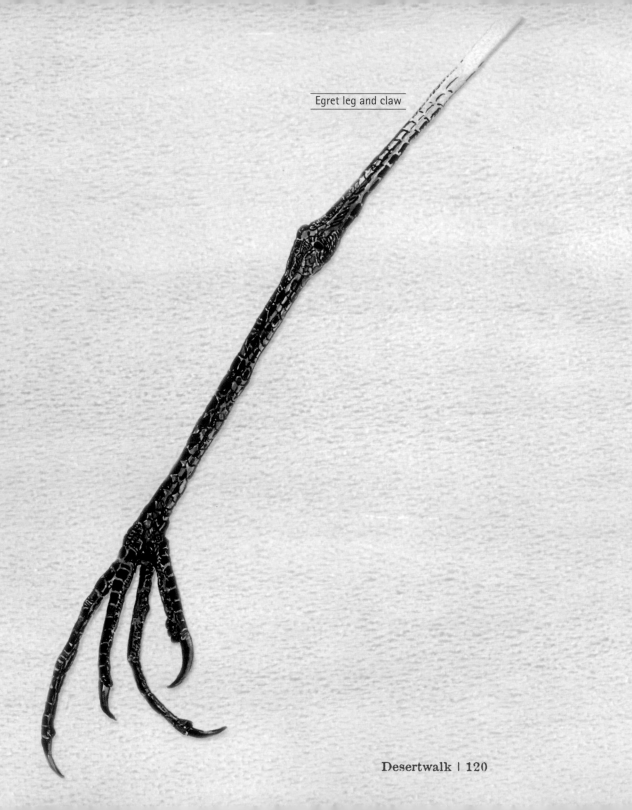

Egret leg and claw

"We are but the ephemera of the moment, the brief custodians..."

- Sterling North

Lazy Days

In the shade of the portal overhang, my dragonfly shaped thermometer registers 112 degrees. Moist, stifling air hangs heavily around my house and yard. Distant mountains fade into the stagnant haze that covers the valley. I feel weak and lethargic. All of my strength is soaked up by the hot, humid air, and breathing seems a chore. It is June first, and the lazy days of summer have arrived.

After a colder than normal spring, the sudden onset of intense heat presents a shock to my system. My body reacts by producing copious amounts of perspiration, but I'm not yet conditioned to handle the heat overload. I'm covered with sweat. Droplets form at my hairline and along the back of my neck. They feel like crawling insects as they dribble down my face and soak into my cotton blouse. If the humidity were low, as is usual in the desert, the dry air would sop up every morsel of sweat almost before it left my pores and the hot weather could be quite tolerable and even comfortable, but today is humid and I feel the heat.

I sit astride the hammock tied between two posts on the *portal* and carefully arrange my body to fit inside its suspended length. I try to doze, but the heat settles down into the hammock's folds like water filling a trough. I use one foot touching the ground to swing back and forth to create a small breeze, but the tightly woven sides of the hammock protect me from feeling any moving air. My body heat radiates against the hammock's sides and bounces back to encase me in a hot nylon cocoon.

I realize the mistake I made by buying this synthetic fabric hammock at a yard sale. I was attracted to the Disney logo with a huge Mickey Mouse character woven into the middle of the fabric. Of course, you can't see the cartoon until you pull open the folds to lie down, which is the part I liked. A surprise hidden in the creases of the hammock awaiting the unsuspecting user is my kind of humor. Now, I know I should have one of those knotted-rope type hammocks instead, where air can get at you from all angles. I'm still learning about desert living.

A whiff of something bad-smelling hits me and it dawns on me that it's the odor from the Salton Sea. Even though this inland body of water, the largest lake in California, is over fifty miles away, when the wind is from the south a stench of rot and decay can permeate the whole Coachella Valley. Usually the smell doesn't get as far as Desert Hot Springs, but if there is a wind from the south it can bring the offensive air to my backyard.

To be fair, I need to point out the Salton Sea doesn't smell all of the time, only when certain conditions exist, such as an isolated fish kill from algae depleting the water of oxygen. As many as 10,000 dead fish were reported in the eastern and northeastern

Mallard feather-both sides.
These ducks are prevalent visitors on desert ponds, artificial lakes and even swimming pools throughout the Coachella Valley.

portions of the sea around Memorial Day. Hot weather fuels the algae blooms, so I can guess that last week's high temperatures encouraged greater than normal algae growth resulting in a plethora of dead fish.

The Salton Sea has no outlet, is fed largely with nitrogen and phosphate-laden water flowing into it from agricultural runoff, and due to rapid evaporation is twenty-five percent saltier than the ocean. In that sense, it is much like the Great Salt Lake in Utah. If we go back four to five million years, the Salton Sink (area covered by Salton Sea at various water levels) was a northern extension of the Gulf of Mexico. Then, during the past two to three million years, sediment buildup separated it from the the ocean and a series of freshwater lakes fed by the Colorado River formed, dried up and reappeared. As the water of the great Colorado shifted its channel over millions of years, it dictated the typography of the Salton Sink, the area where the Salton Sea lies today.

The most recent of these lakes was known as Lake Cahuilla (ku-WEE-yah), named after the native people who lived on its shores. Its highest water level occurred sometime between the years 1660 and 1680. We know this by the white bathtub ring of crusty tufa, formed from calcium carbonate deposits, etched on the surrounding bedrock at forty-two feet above ground level.

As the last of the ancient freshwater lakes, its life-giving waters allowed people to live in the desert. Fish traps consisting of a series of rectangular-shaped stone basins are still in evidence along the various high-water levels of old Lake Cahuilla. Most likely the traps were used by Desert Cahuilla Indians in the winter months, since during the hot summer season they migrated higher into the mountains.

On a geology field trip I treated myself to one Saturday, we parked our cars on the side of a road and wandered the

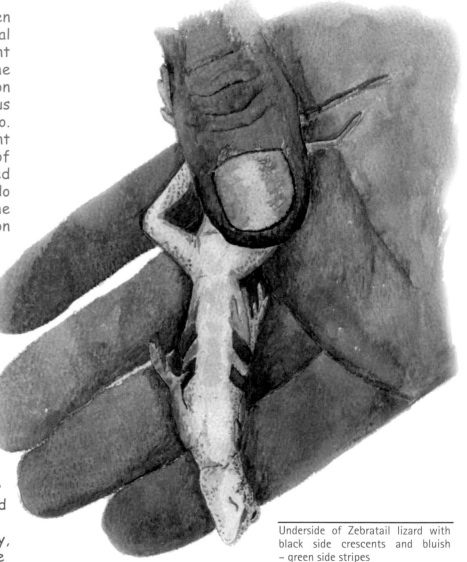

Underside of Zebratail lizard with black side crescents and bluish – green side stripes

adjacent sandy field picking up delicate white clam shells. We were walking on an ancient beach, once part of Lake Cahuilla, now twenty to thirty miles from any natural water. I was fascinated with the concept of a beach in the middle of a waterless desert.

As I scanned the ground for a perfect shell specimen, I came upon a broken piece of pottery, a shard from another time. Several more, half-buried in the ancient beach strata, caught my eye as I ambled over the shell-speckled sands. The beach gained even more importance in my mind as I realized these remnants of an earlier people confirmed the dependence on Lake Cahuilla by those who called the desert home.

Probably the most intriguing story of the Salton Sea is the myth of the sixteenth century Spanish galleon that may lie buried in its sands. As the legend goes, the ship sailed up from the Gulf of California into Lake Cahuilla, which at that time extended 115 miles from the city of Indio into Mexico and was larger than the state of Delaware. It is said

a landslide or sandbar blocked the vessel's path of return to the sea. The crew had no choice but to abandon ship and walk out across the desert. In time, drifting sands covered the galleon, which may remain in its secret burial chamber to this day. Some say the ship was loaded with pearls and gold and many have gone to seek it, returning with stories of old ship timbers and tattered sails, but no proof other than their intriguing tales.

In reality, it would have been possible to sail this sea route, and some accounts capture the imagination more than others. In a 1933 book, *The Journey of the Flame,* by Antonio de Fierro Blanco, the author writes about a mule driver with the Spanish explorer Juan Baptista de Anza in 1774 who stumbled across a cache of pearls in a ship partially buried in the desert sands. He took all he could carry, deserted Baptista's party and went his own way. The rest of his life was reportedly spent searching for the lost ship. This account came from a man who, at the age of 104 related the story to Blanco, claiming the mule driver had confided in him and he had kept the man's secret for many decades.

Feathers from one of many birds found at Salton Sea

Whether a Spanish galleon lies beneath the desert in the Salton Sea area or not, we do know a World War II Avenger torpedo bomber rests under the salty waters. It was discovered in 1999 by divers searching for a missing Piper Cherokee. According to Navy records, the Salton Sea has claimed over three dozen men, four Wildcat airplanes, two Corsairs, two Hellcats, four patrol planes, two Helldivers and ten Avengers, all of which crashed into the waters during training exercises.

The colorful history of the Salton Sea is sometimes forgotten when the odor from decaying fish permeates the Coachella Valley air. Once an important source for fish, water and recreation, restaurants and resorts flourished along its shores. In the 1940's, movie stars water-skied and raced over the inland waters in their jazzy wooden Chris Crafts.

Only recently has this remaining part of the much larger ancient Lake Cahuilla fallen on hard times. It seems a shame to have such a bad reputation now, when in the past it was the life-giving feature of the Coachella Valley. Mullet, one of the salt water fish that migrated from the Gulf of California into the Salton Sea via the Colorado River during the early 1900's, along with corvina and other game fish, were once an important part of the recreational use of the Salton Sea. Now the fish suffocate and create a nuisance odor.

Studies are going on and plans are discussed on how to heal the Salton Sea and bring it back to the attractive recreational and ecological status it once had, when fishing and vacationing were major activities on its shores. So, while it may have a bad smell today, it continues to be an important part of our life-giving ecosystem. Functioning as a major stop-off for migrating birds and refuge for wildlife is still a most valuable feature. People could live here in the past because of the fresh water, fish and wildlife. While we don't subsist today on fish and hunting small animals, water remains our most important resource.

I would rather not be assaulted with the odor of rotten fish, but I realize I'm part of the problem that created it. I buy and eat vegetables and other food products grown on agricultural land that drains into the Salton Sea, clogging it with nutrients that produce algae blooms. We brought about the current situation by diverting Colorado River water for drinking and enabling more development in Southern California, so it is up to us to solve the problem we created. I hope for solutions soon from creative minds who are working to allow agriculture and a viable inland sea, where people may once again use its resources for sustenance as well as recreation. The smell today is a reminder of the problem we must solve in a way consistent with the vast geological history of the Salton Sink.

As my olfactory senses tire, the fetid odor seems less offensive. Still overly warm but finally comfortable in the hammock, I decide a short nap would compliment this lazy summer afternoon. With my eyes closed, and the hammock swaying as gently as a baby's cradle, I begin to drift off. A pesky fly lands on my bare leg. I wave it away only to have it circle and alight on my arm. Another perches on my check. They don't bite, but they tickle and annoy. I give up and go in the house away from the heat and the flies and the bad smell. Today, I will enjoy the lazy days of summer inside.

Light version of Western Whiptail lizard.

"Life is a series of surprises"

- Emerson

Visiting Wildlife

Arriving home from a month in the mountains, where we went to escape the heat and monsoon humidity of August in the desert, I try to settle into my usual household routine. My vacation-disoriented mind and body refuse to cooperate, so I ignore the stack of mail piled on the kitchen island. *Maybe later,* I think. Taking care of the pile of laundry sitting next to the washing machine doesn't appeal to me either, but I can probably handle putting my office in order.

The first thing I need to do is reconnect my laptop computer to all the other gadgets it uses. I swivel my chair around to face the cabinet behind my desk, and reach down to pull out the rolling shelf that holds my printer. Nestled in the front corner, only a few inches from my hand, is a flat, round disc, about the size of water glass base. It has the look of a very pale coiled-up snake, but is so obviously only a plaster cast that I smile thinking what a poor replica it is.

Ah ha, I think, *my daughter, Holly, set that bad snake replica there as a joke.* She has been tending to the house during our absence, and knows I am squeamish about snakes. We often kid about how I seem to be the person who catches sight of them more often than anyone else. She, on the other hand, doesn't mind crawling reptiles and will pick up and handle non-venomous ones.

She even has a fake snake in her garden. It's made of hard plastic that looks fairly realistic. We laugh because it moves around and shows up in different places, sometimes lying upside down. Apparently birds and other nocturnal feeders are fooled enough to pick it up for a tasty meal. When they find it's not edible, they drop it, generally away from where they found it. So the fake snake travels all over the garden.

I'm not so gullible and can recognize a fake when I see one. I reach out to pick up the plaster cast on my printer shelf. But just before my hand touches it, a teeny bit of caution creeps into my head and I think maybe I should just be sure it is plaster. I pick up an envelope lying on top of a stack of papers and use it to poke at the side of the fake snake. The folded paper point pushes easily into the soft coiled object. My hand involuntarily jumps away.

But even after being poked, there is no movement or sign of life. So this is not a plaster cast, but a soft rubber or plastic imitation. Nature companies make such good replicas.

Suddenly, panic replaces caution as I think, *What if it is a real snake?* I run to find my husband. He's talking on the phone in his office, sounding rather serious and motions for me to wait. By now my heart is thumping with anxiety. If it's real, will it crawl away while I'm out of the room and I won't know where it went? That is by far one of my worst nightmares - a snake loose in the house.

I tear into the pantry to grab a clear plastic cup that can be used to clamp down over the coiled object to trap it in place, while I yell for my husband to come as soon as possible. I run back to my office hoping if the snake is alive it will still be where I can see it. It hasn't moved. I breathe a small sigh of relief, but wonder how silly I'm going to feel when he finds it's a fake, laughs and says, "You really fell for this one."

With cup in hand ready for use, I wait for Court to save me from a reptile or a replica, I don't know which. He comes within a few minutes, which seem like forever, and takes the cup from my hand. He places it over the whitish-grey coil, but while trying to fit it down tightly against the shelf, the plaster replica raises its head and slithers away into a dark recess of the corner cupboard.

Sidewinder tracks

Now I'm terrified, worrying it will find a crack or niche to hide in, we won't be able to get it out, and I will have a snake loose in my office. And this is not just any snake, its heart-shaped head with small triangular horn-like projections easily identifies it as a small sidewinder rattlesnake.

In spite of the fact the snake has really unsettled me, I am very good about remaining sensible and able to act rationally in crisis situations. So while Court keeps his eye on the reptile, I go back to the pantry and find a flashlight, long handled barbecue tongs, and an empty metal cookie box with cover.

When I return, he shines the light into the dark cavity behind the printer, reaches in with the tongs, picks up the snake and drops it in the box as I slam on the tight-fitting lid. I am saved by my brave knight, Sir Courtney, my husband. I am so relieved. Even though the snake is small, only about eight inches long, (my husband says ten to twelve) it could be dangerous. I've read that baby snakes cannot control their venom and therefore every bite carries the full load, whereas adult snakes are sometimes known to bite with no venom or only a little. The truth of this, I don't know, and don't care to find out, since I intend to avoid bites from reptiles of any size.

I've never even seen a live sidewinder before, only its distinctive tracks in the sand when I go walking in the desert. I had assumed they were darker colored but, when I think about it, the very pale hue of the snake matches the light grey granitic sand outside.

With the sidewinder captured and safely imprisoned in a tall metal wastebasket on the patio, any danger from a rattlesnake in the house is over, but the question is, how did it get in? Court suggests it probably crawled in through an open door while our pine floors were being sanded and refinished during the month we spent in the mountains. The house was empty but cool, the dog and the inside cat were both with us, so a dim, quiet house would have been a great place for a snake to hang out. The explanation seems reasonable and, in spite of the adrenalin still coursing through my body, I try to calm down and put the incident behind me.

More than anything, though, I can't help but think about how I almost tried to pick up a venomous snake. I shudder and try not to go any further with that image. The crisis is over. Tomorrow the sidewinder can be released into the wild far, far away from the house. I still feel a little "shaken" but all seems well and I spend the rest of my day with the business of unpacking, now an easy job with the help of all the adrenalin released during the snake incident.

At bedtime, when I finish brushing my teeth and turn out the bathroom light, Court is already engrossed in a new book and settled comfortably in bed among the pillows. I cross the dark bedroom floor with only a dim glow from my husband's reading lamp to illuminate the room. The fur of a black and white cow skin rug at the foot of our bed feels gentle on my feet and, after a rather stressful day, I'm ready to snuggle into fresh sheets and soft pillows. I bend down in the semi-dark room to pick up a scrap of ribbon or yarn lying in an "S" shape on the white background of the rug. Before I actually touch the object in the dim light, I realize it's another small sidewinder.

"It's another snake!" I shout at Court, who leaps out of bed and stands with me to look, both of us with disbelief. The snake quickly flips sideways and disappears under the fat round tail of our big dog who is lying nearby on the cool tile floor. Before we can think of what to do, it slithers out from under him and disappears underneath the dog bed a few feet away.

"You stay and watch," I say, "and I'll get the tools." I run out to the kitchen in my bare feet straining to look at the floor in the darkness, almost expecting to step on something squishy. I grab the clear plastic cup, barbecue tongs, metal box and a broom. This time I need a broom so that if the snake tries to crawl away I can stop or direct its motion with the broom bristles. I really, really don't want the snake to crawl under my bed.

When we lift up the edge of the dog bed and flip it aside, the snake is coiled in a small circle just like the one found in my office, except that its head is up and alert. In a motion so swift I almost don't see it, Court clamps the cup down over the coiled rattler. I rip off the stiff cover of a magazine and Court eases it under the snake, trapping it in the plastic glass. With the magazine cover as a lid, he picks up the cup holding the snake and dumps the reptile into the metal box. For the second time in one day, I quickly clamp down the cover.

Thrown off balance by the first sidewinder, the second one leaves me with real dread. How many more are there in the house? Are these babies from a nest of many? What next?

Our bed is elevated on a platform so it seems a safe place to spend the night. Sir Courtney, my brave knight and savior, assures me that in the morning he will go room by room and search in every nook and crevice, and if there are more snakes in the house he will find them.

The next day, after over an hour on hands and knees and stomach with a flashlight shining under and into every possible hiding place imaginable, the house is pronounced safe.

It is then we notice that Geronimo, the dog, has one hind leg and paw swollen to three times its normal size. Again, in disbelief, we look at one another and realize at the same time that Geronimo must have been bitten last night by the snake in the bedroom. He could have stepped on it earlier or it may have struck when it crawled under his

common bat *(Myotis californicus)* Bats are not to be feared, they eat tons of insects.

tail. I don't think the dog was aware of the bite since he didn't even notice the snake. He doesn't seem to be in pain and walks around as usual except for having a little trouble lying down on the affected side. Court whisks him off to the vet.

The doctor gives antibiotics to Geronimo and tells us that most dogs recover from rattlesnake bites, so ours should be fine. The antibiotics are to guard against infection, since a rattlesnake's mouth is full of bacteria. The swelling, he says, should go down in three to four days.

A week later, Geronimo has recovered, his paws are all the same size, no more snakes have turned up in or out of the house and I can now look at the experience with a different perspective. In telling my story to a friend in Rancho Mirage, she relayed her experiences with several big fat diamondback rattlesnakes that turned up inside her patio. One was so heavy the animal control person she called, struggled to lift it into the plastic trash can he'd brought to contain the snake and carry it away.

With that ugly picture in my mind, I've stopped making so much out of my small-snake encounter. However, I can't seem to walk anywhere in the house without looking at the floor. I'm especially careful walking barefoot. I don't know how long this obsession will last, but maybe it's not a bad habit.

If I want to live surrounded by nature, I have to accept all parts of the natural world. I can't pick and choose only those I think are cute or attractive. That is the hardest lesson to learn. A touch of nature, a brief but safe view, may be fascinating. But the reality of the natural world is the magnificent interaction of it all, including the cute and the ugly and the dangerous. I wouldn't want it any other way.

According to *A Natural History of the Sonoran Desert,* published by the Arizona Sonoran Desert Museum, sidewinders *(Crotalus cerates)* breed in the spring. Five to eighteen young snakes six to eight inches long are born alive in late summer or early fall. Sidewinders are active year-round where it is warm, and shelter during the heat of the day in an animal burrow or by burying themselves in the sand, often under a creosote bush. I would like to add that they may also choose a cool, empty house if it is available.

"Sidewinders move forward by throwing parts of their body sideways above ground. This results in a series of curved tracks with space between and allows them to move more easily over loose sand."

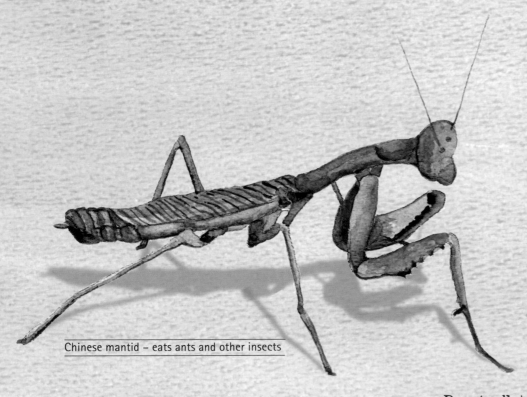

Chinese mantid – eats ants and other insects

Wonder is the beginning of wisdom.

- Greek proverb

Desert Reflections

With sun barely peeking above the horizon, desert light is still pale. I walk briskly with my light jacket zipped up to keep out crisp morning air still lingering from the chilly night. After a colder than usual winter with ample rainfall, spring continues in a cooler than normal mode making mornings a good time for a refreshing walk.

By the time Geronimo and I cover about half a mile, full sunlight fills the eastern sky and my morning world is infused with a golden-yellow glow. Pinpoints of glitter speckle the sand ahead and coat Geronimo's brown fur with tips of silver. The ground looks as if a gigantic mirror shattered in space and cast its thousands of fragments over the landscape. For a short time while the sun is at a low angle in the sky, my desert vista is clothed in sequin-studded robes.

As I approach a spot of glitter, expecting a shard of glass or shiny metal, I find instead a small particle of granite with a smooth polished surface reflecting the rising sun. Off to my left and right, the sand looks normal. Only ahead of me, as I face the sun, is the angle of its rays just right to bounce off smooth stones and fill my forward view with pin pricks of brilliance. I am often fooled by a glimmer

A Phacelia from the waterleaf family

I think is glass. Sometimes it turns out to be a stiff leaf turned at just the right angle to reflect light into my eyes. Sometimes it's only a dry twig with an exposed shiny surface where its bark has peeled away. Green palm fronds sway in the gentle breeze. Their smooth, glossy surfaces catch the low morning sun and wave a greeting with twinkling tips giving a festively dressed appearance, as if for a party.

Desert adapted plants frequently conserve water by developing hard outer coverings that prevent evaporation, and it's these sturdy parts that also reflect light. I never thought of the desert as a glittery place, but on most mornings as the sun begins its arc across the sky, it gives every smooth, hard surface a glint of radiance, a sprinkling of brightness that settles like dust motes on dunes and bushes.

It draws me forward. I'm always wanting to see what lies ahead, always thinking a treasure awaits further on. Like the mythical pot of gold at the end of a rainbow, the search draws me, but the prize remains ahead, I never reach it.

A particularly large shiny spot draws my attention, but when I get close, I see it is a small white stone, no larger than half the palm of my hand. I pick it up and examine its surface covered with multiple facets so glossy they feel as if they are oiled.

Stones like this are called ventifacts. *Vent* is French for wind, a ventifact is made by wind. Burnished to a high sheen by blowing sand particles, these wind-fashioned rocks can be clues to prevailing wind directions. One collection of ventifacts containing over 3,000 examples, each one marked with the compass orientation of where it was found, is used as the basis for fundamental wind erosion and aerodynamic studies.

It takes an inquisitive mind to learn from subtleties so generally overlooked. If I were doing research, I would investigate the time involved in creating a ventifact. Obviously it depends upon how hard and how often the wind blows, but I would

Milkvetch leaves

like to know if it took 10, 100 or 1,000 years to create the polish on the stone I hold in my hand.

When I was little we called these polished rocks "touch stones," because they felt so nice to the touch. As kids we'd each have a favorite to carry around in our pocket as something to run our fingers across and to think of as a good luck piece. Mine was never as shiny or pretty as the ones my older brothers had. I looked up to them and followed them around like a loyal little puppy dog.

Now, I run my thumb and forefinger back and forth over the surface of the stone I picked up this morning. The sensation I get from the ventifact is sensuous and mesmerizing. I feel lucky to have found it. I look westward towards the source of the prevailing winds and whisper, "Thank you for this small token as a reminder of your power."

With the stone grasped in my fist, I think of how canyons, mountains, dunes make up the desert landscape; all are sculpted by wind and water. But it is this small ventifact, as a part of the sequin-studded desert that speaks to me this morning.

Nature's glitter, sparkling as dawn lights up the awakening land and in late afternoon when the angle of the sun is low, is not an intrusion on the landscape like broken glass or metal scraps.

The reflections nature reveals tell their own story. They sing of sand-carrying winds polishing rocks, of turbulent flood waters rolling stones to new locations, of mountain rain raging down canyons and digging arroyos into desert flatlands. Everywhere are small reminders of powerful natural forces shaping, sculpting and altering the landscape.

As the sun continues up its scheduled path, the cool air begins to warm. I take off my jacket and tie its sleeves around my waist. Geronimo is panting, so we will walk home past one of the ponds where he can get a drink.

With such a beginning, born of the light that gives life, the day ahead can only be spectacular. As I go about my daily tasks, the glitter of early morning turns into yellow sunlight adding cheer to all I see. It lights my way into today's journey and entices me ever forward. That is enough. I need nothing more.

Ventifact – smoothed and polished by wind blown sand.

California Milkvetch, an endangered species

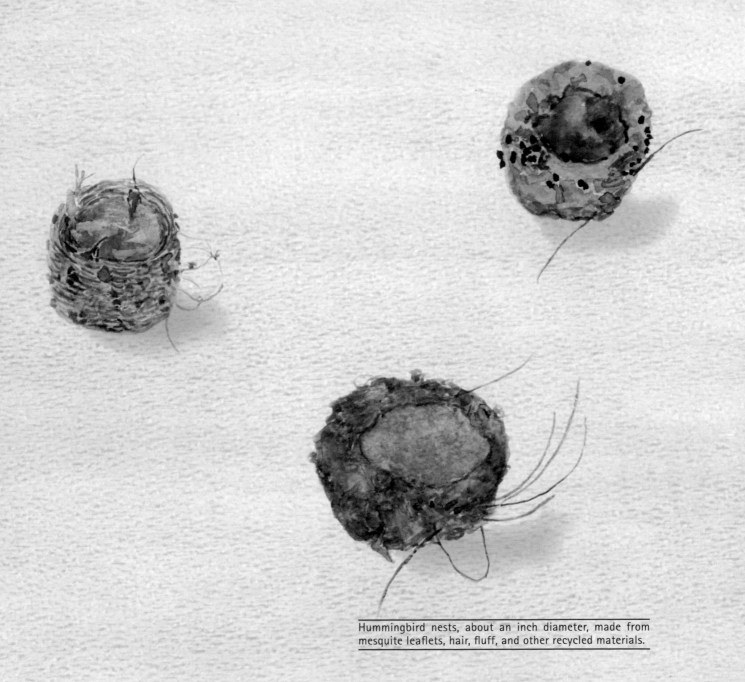

Hummingbird nests, about an inch diameter, made from mesquite leaflets, hair, fluff, and other recycled materials.

"Our task must be to free ourselves...by widening our circle of compassion to embrace all living creatures and the whole of nature and its beauty"

- Albert Einstein

Desert Recyclers

While walking along a sandy strip between clumps of creosote bush, a strange looking stick catches my attention. I pick it up for a closer look and wonder what produced the hard mud-like substance covering its entire surface. It looks like sand glued around a twig forming a perfectly smooth coating. On the ground are several other small, inch-long pieces of hollow tubes. I select one, wrap it carefully in a tissue, and put it in my pack to take home.

Later, after doing some research on insects, I discover the hard sand coverings are "soil tubes" made by termites. They use saliva to cement soil particles together in tunnels, around objects and as a part of their mound. In the desert, termites live underground or in decaying wood and are often mistaken for ants. At only one-eighth to seven-sixteenths of an inch long, they are not easily seen. I have sometimes picked up pieces of dead wood on my walks and watched as tiny disturbed insects ran wildly about, but at the time I had no idea they were termites. Nor did I understand their extreme importance to desert ecology.

Termites are recyclers of waste cellulose, that is wood debris, dead grasses and plants, cactus skeletons and dung. In wetter areas, fungi break down wood and plant material, returning it to the soil as enriching nutrients. Even though I've found some fungi growing in the desert, it is not enough to do the same job as in wetter climates, so termites fulfill the recycling function instead.

But even termites can't do it alone. They have a symbiotic relationship with protozoans who live in their digestive system. The termites bite off chunks of wood they can't digest and the protozoans turn it into sugar which the termites can absorb, and ultimately it returns to the soil as nutrients for growing new plants.

To make the story of termites even more bizarre,
young termites are born without the protozoans, and have to acquire them by eating the feces of their older members. However, this may not be quite as gross as it sounds since the feces has already been changed to sugar and nutrients by the protozoans.

Without termites and protozoans doing their recycling job, dead wood, plant material and dung would build up in a layer so thick, there would be no space for new plants to grow and no enriched soil for them to grow in. Without termites, the desert would be uninhabitable - a vast wasteland. Who knew those busy little critters are doing us such an enormous favor? All my life I have been led to believe termites prey upon us by eating the wood of our homes. Now I realize they can't be expected to know which wood to eat and which to ignore.

One estimate goes so far as to suggest that without termites, twenty percent of the surface of the land would be smothered in dung over a fifty year period. That thought is enough for me to take a more tolerant attitude toward these little guys. So if they happen to choose unwisely and attack the timbers of my house, I can't blame them since they are merely doing their job. I had always thought of them as destructive insects. I never would have guessed they are a

Leaf-cutter ants made these hollow tubes from bougainvillea leaves and bracts

necessary element in maintaining the environment. I should have realized there was more to the termite story, since Mother nature seems to know what she's doing, even if we don't have a complete understanding.

As social insects, termites have a complex society with division of labor that includes caring for their young as well as some of the same social structure we utilize. Each termite colony has a queen, king, workers and soldiers. These groups are called castes, and when the colony reaches a maximum size it produces nymphs that will ultimately become any one of the four castes, depending upon what is needed. How convenient is that?

Nymphs may also fly off and colonize a new area. Soldiers have enlarged heads with strong jaws so they can do guard duty, workers are white in color and collect food, which includes feeding the soldiers and queen and king. The king and large wingless queen take care of egg production. In the tropics, a queen may be as thick as a sausage and as big as four inches long. So swollen with eggs she is immobile, workers feed and groom her.

I was astounded to discover there are over 2,000 different species of termites throughout the world and over forty in North America. Only three main types are found in the desert. Because they live underground or under decaying wood, they remain well hidden from the casual observer.

In other parts of the world, termites build complex structures, ranging

Seed pods from a back yard tree

from steeple-like mounds twenty feet high, with built-in air conditioning channels in the outer walls, to an Australian species that constructs a compass mound. Its walls may be as much as ten feet long and twelve feet high, and nearly always point north-south. The four-feet thick flat sides face east and west. How these tiny bugs can figure out directions is unknown, but some day when we finally figure it out, I'm confident it will be another "gee whiz" discovery that may add significantly to our own lives.

These highly specialized insects have had countless generations to adapt to specific climates and landforms. Evidence of termites exists from 100 million years ago during the age of dinosaurs. They may even have been around during the Cambrian explosion of life, 600 million years ago, when precursors of all animal life developed.

I now know more about termites than I would have ever thought possible or desirable, but I also know we have much to learn from termites. For some reason I don't understand, the desert is viewed by many people as a dumping ground for trash. Instead of making the effort to recycle or get rid of refuse in the proper manner, there are those who haul it to vacant land and dump it. Bed springs, old appliances, glass and metal

> "The balance and beauty of the natural desert, which if left alone, can sustain itself, get rid of its own refuse and create new beauty each season."

don't break down in nature and there are no unseen recyclers like termites for these items, so they must be disposed of by means other than natural breakdown and decay.

I get riled up with dumpers because I see on a daily basis, the balance and beauty of the natural desert, which if left alone, can sustain itself, get rid of its own refuse and create new beauty each season. If tiny one-eighth-inch termites can keep this land unsullied, how is it that our highly industrialized, intelligent, inventive civilization cannot respect and maintain the same standards as a termite?

It makes me wonder what caste these irresponsible people would be if they were in termite society. Obviously, those who litter have little respect for desert beauty and even less knowledge of how nature serves us.

The more I learn about the desert, the more I marvel at every aspect of it. So much not understood is like the termites: unseen but doing an important and necessary job.

As I continue to explore and learn, my appreciation continues to soar. My greatest hope is that I can transfer some of that understanding to others who have not been as fortunate as I to walk the desert sands in all seasons.

Sections of a cholla cactus skeleton on its way to being recycled back into the soil.

"Life is not measured by the number of breaths we take,
but by the moments that take our breath away."

- Unknown

The Searchers

Yesterday, my husband came out to the *portal* and found me lying on a lounge chair staring up at the sky. I had to convince him I was feeling fine and simply taking in the blue, blue color of the world above me. This was a desert sky, clear and compelling, magnetic in its reach. *It must be the way the heavens looked,* I thought, *before man took over the earth, before greenhouse gas emissions, before cars, factories, before coal and gas and other pollutants sullied the air.* The brilliant, sapphire, azure, aquamarine, or some blue I can't describe in words, was so vivid, I felt as if I might drift upward into the intense color and dissolve into its sea of blue.

Before I moved to the desert, when I lived where green trees, shrubs, flowers and lawns grew in profusion, I thought the pale pastels of desert paintings looked anemic and washed out. I was used to stronger greens and primary colors surrounding me on ground level but above was an atmosphere tinted gray with moisture-laden air. Now, living in the desert, the opposite is the rule. The land is layered with pastel tints and pale, often grayed, colors but the sky above is a striking electric blue.

These clear skies are one of the alluring attributes of the desert. Other advantages of desert living are not so easily defined. Many are mysteries hidden from the casual observer's eye, yet they call longingly, and those of us who hear are won over so completely we are caught forever like flies on fly paper.

The desert has a way of attracting those people searching

cultivated cactus

for more of what they want out of life. Some gravitate here for wide-open remote locations where they can be themselves and invent their own lifestyle. Leonard Knight was one of those who came to the desert over twenty years ago and camped on a piece of land next to Slab City and the tiny town of Niland near the Salton Sea. Slab City, itself, is a desert phenomenon, a place where snowbirds (people leaving cold climates during winter months) bring their motor homes and trailers to spend the winter on concrete slabs remaining from General Patton's training camp during World War II.

Leonard Knight didn't even have a trailer. He just parked his truck on a five acre plot of desert land and began building his monument celebrating his love of God. Using native clay, hay, an existing mound of sand and cans of salvaged paint, he created Salvation Mountain, a gigantic mound painted with every color imaginable. Emblazoned across the front, in white letters impossible to miss is his message, **God is Love.** Now, years later, Salvation Mountain has grown to include whole rooms, caves and eccentric pathways to explore. It is never finished; Leonard just keeps on working every day.

When my husband and I and some friends went to see it on what we call a "lolly," that is heading off with no specific plans, just open to whatever adventure may arise, we parked our car, stepped out of comfortable air-conditioning into stifling heat, and headed towards a rock-outlined path leading to the gaudy, painted, two-story high mound. An elderly man dressed in brown pants and a wrinkled flowered shirt approached us. My first thought was, *Oh, oh, we're going* to have to deal with a weirdo and be hit up for money. But Leonard Knight, we discovered, is a gentleman and he doesn't expect to be paid. He showed us around, answered our questions and, when we offered him money, he made it clear we were not obligated in any way.

There are days Leonard has over 100 visitors, tour buses full of curious people and, while he accepts donations, no one is ever asked to pay to tour Salvation Mountain. Paint donations, however, are always welcome, since over the years he has used up thousands of gallons of leftover paint.

At one time, Leonard was about to be evicted from the government-owned property he simply "adopted." But his friends and fellow artists supported him so vigorously his religious art monument was allowed to remain. Now the site is recognized as folk art, has been entered into the congressional record as a national treasure, and is described as a unique and visionary sculpture in a dry, desolate landscape.

This same type of desolate landscape attracted another unusual artist in the Twenty-nine Palms area of the high desert. Noah Purifoy brought his found-object, collage talent to a flat, open sandy field where he put together sculptures and assemblages from salvaged materials. Porcelain toilet bowls, wire mesh, old clothing, building materials, vacuum cleaners, and countless objects impossible to list, fill the acreage with ingenious structures and sculptures.

Noah left Los Angeles and the school he started at the Watts Towers (another eccentric construction of metal and ceramics by Simon Rodia) to build his artistic sculptures in the desert, where land was cheap and he could work uninterrupted. When I met Noah, he was confined to a wheelchair and students were on hand to help conserve his outdoor works of art.

Like Leonard Knight, Noah was a nice person, willing to talk about his art and happy to welcome viewers. Not long after our visit, he passed away. As a unique artist who viewed the world in ways that stimulate insightful thoughts about our culture, I cannot view his works without continuously shaking my head and realizing Noah Purifoy was truly a visionary. His perceptions of our throw-away society make me dig deeply into rethinking my own view of life

In contrast to the colorful works of Leonard Knight and complicated iconography of Noah Purifoy, the remains of a simple rustic stone house still stand in Long Canyon on the Desert Hot Springs side of the Little San Bernardino Mountains. The round trip hike to reach it is close to eight miles. When Bill Simmons, who later became known as Chuckwalla Bill, built the house entirely of stone, there was water nearby which has since dried up. He lived there for many years with his lady friend, Grace Mazeris, and came into town only occasionally for supplies. Prior to the stone house, Chuckwalla Bill lived for a while in a cave-like recess located in a remote canyon near Boulder City, Nevada and often with friends for whom he cooked and did odd jobs.

Everyone seemed to like him, thought he was impeccably honest and viewed him as a very decent man who knew what he wanted, was free to live the way he liked and willing to pay the penalties for doing it. Born during the Industrial Revolution, he rejected factory jobs and urban living. By traveling west and settling wherever he could in the unknown, unpopulated, great American desert, he became a part of the land, a fixture that belonged, a person caught by the desert spell and kept entrapped in its net of solitude.

He was a friend of Cabot Yerxa who also migrated from the east and spent a large part of his life building a 5,000 square foot Indian style pueblo dwelling with 35 rooms, 150 windows, and 65 doors, none of which are alike. He used salvaged materials scavenged from the desert and made his own adobe from native clay mixed with concrete. Until he dug his first well which yielded scalding hot water, he and his mule, Merry Christmas, carried water from seven miles away at Garnet, now the train station in the west end of the Coachella Valley.

One might think Cabot Yerxa was just an eccentric "Desert Rat," but, in truth, he was a cultured, highly talented man. His engraved calling card is but one one the many indications of the remarkable diverse aspects of the Cabot who knew Teddy Roosevelt, wrote for a New York newspaper, was a 32nd degree Mason and used his training from the Julian Art Academy in France to produce a large body of early desert paintings. Unable to buy paints and canvas, he painted on boards and mixed his own colors with formulas he devised using desert herbs and minerals.

As one of the earliest residents of Desert Hot Springs, he is credited with the discovery of the hot mineral water, although Indians inhabiting the area had known of it for hundreds of years. Mineral water at 135 degrees F. still bubbles up from the sand at Two Bunch Palms, a nearby spa resort that attracts visitors from all over the world.

Cabot Yerxa, after living elsewhere, including several years selling cigars in Alaska during the Gold Rush when he was only nineteen years old, and serving in the army in World War I, was pulled back to the desert to spend the rest of his life constructing his monumental home honoring the Southwestern pueblo Indians. His hand-built pueblo style house and most of his possessions remain intact today as Cabot's Pueblo Museum in Desert Hot Springs.

As I think about these adventurous people who chose the solitude and serenity of the desert for the place to spend their lives, I wonder if the move my husband and I made is much different. Even though we have all the modern conveniences and our physical lives are very comfortable, the same lure of the desert has captured us, just as it reeled in the earlier settlers I've described.

That first blue sky we experienced pulled us like iron filings to a magnet. We could not wrench free and were caught in the spell of desert magic. As we walked along warm sands exploring smoke tree-filled washes and gazed at nearby mountains protecting the valley in all directions, a sense of belonging nipped at our heels and wouldn't be quiet.

I have come to realize that we are building our own monument as we clear and mark paths, extend the gardens farther and farther out from our house, construct walls and ponds, ramadas and rest areas. Just as Cabot continued to build until the day he died, I'm sure we will undertake new projects and never be finished. The fun is in the doing and we will keep on "doing" until we are no more.

Could it be the vast desert holds the secret to living a contented life that is felt, but not easily described? Eskimos have many words for types of snow because so much of their environment consists of it. Perhaps desert living for our culture is too new to have developed the precise and varied vocabulary for expressing what we feel here. Some, like Leonard Knight, Bill Simmons, Cabot Yerxa, and Noah Purifoy may have understood better than others.

I think the best of all worlds is to be free to choose the place that suits me and to give in when it reaches out and envelops me with its compelling aura. Whether I can articulate its benefits or not, it's what I have chosen because I know instinctively the serenity and peace I experience living amidst nature is what I need to feel alive and content.

Brittlebush (*Encelia farinosa*) – common desert native

"Aspire to live in awe!"

from a fortune cookie

Inchworm in the Sky

Instead of a walk this morning, I get up extra early while it's still dark outside, dress in something nice instead of my usual shorts and shirt, and hurry out to a breakfast meeting. When no one else shows up, I leave the restaurant and head for home feeling annoyed with myself for getting the date wrong. While I think about whether I'm in the mood to take a late walk or just admit I wasted part of my morning, a resplendent act of nature brings me to my senses.

Facing west as I turn the corner, a pillar of colors glowing with luminescence rises from the ground and shines like a jeweled brooch against the dark-shadowed backdrop of Mt. San Jacinto. A rainbow just beginning to form with all seven colors – red – orange - yellow – green – blue - indigo and violet, shimmers vividly in the pale morning sky. I am momentarily stunned. When I remember to breathe, I pull over to the curb and turn off the ignition. Just sitting and treating my eyes to this unexpected gift on a raincloud-studded morning is enough to lift my spirits and make me glad to be alive.

I roll down my car window and inhale cool, damp, desert air, enhanced by an overnight rain, herbal fragrances, and the distinctive tangy scent of creosote bushes mingled with the smell of moist sand. As I sit and look at the base of the mountain, bedecked with its tower of shimmering rainbow colors, tinges of red-orange and yellow begin crawling upwards across the sky, and within a few moments all seven rainbow hues appear in a gigantic half-circle across the purple-gray heavens. The rainbow, no longer a tower, but instead, a complete arc across the sky, lasts only about a minute, then it is gone. I sit in my car, filled with reverence for a glorious event created entirely by a combination of natural conditions.

It was my husband who taught me why and how rainbows develop, so I understand this is a perfectly natural event and not some mystical sign. To begin with, there must be excessive moisture in the air and the sun has to be behind the observer. A rainbow forms when sunlight is spread into its spectrum of colors through water droplets acting as prisms to separate light into its individual colors.

For me to really understand this natural phenomenon, I have to visualize a ray of light hitting a drop of water, bending at its refraction angle as it passes through the droplet, and then reflecting off the back of the water droplet to my eye. Since each color making up white light has a different degree of refraction, the individual bands of color are separated out and appear in the form of a rainbow.

I like knowing the scientific reasons rainbows occur, but it's experiencing them that captivates me. While every rainbow I have ever seen was special, in the desert they always seem more monumental than anywhere else. It may have to do with the way desert rainbows stretch across the horizon without tall buildings to impede the view. Or it may just be that every rainbow has its own allure far beyond its physical explanation, and I am at a stage in life when I take more notice then I did in the past. Yet, I can't imagine there is a soul on earth who can look away with disinterest when seeing a band of reds, yellows, purples and greens painting the sky with a massive and perfect half circle.

This morning's rainbow, both striking and ephemeral, pulls me into the world of rainbow mythology. The illusion of a colorful sky bridge, appearing suddenly as if by magic and fading away softly, has always fascinated people and been the origin of myths and stories. Early civilizations, lacking scientific knowledge, attached great importance to an event as overwhelmingly beautiful and illusive as a rainbow. They recorded them in petroglyphs carved into rocks and used them as symbols of their beliefs.

It was back in the late 1800's that Lieutenant Colonel Garrick Mallery, one of the few people at that time who took an interest in rock art, coined the terms *pictographs* for rock paintings and *petroglyphs* for rock carvings. In 1893, he assembled a report on *Picture Writing of the American*

Indians which is still considered valuable today, since it describes rock writing sites no longer in existence.

However, his interpretation of the rainbow symbol seems a bit unusual. He described it as a deified animal having the attributes of a human being, yet also the body and some of the functions of a measuring or inch worm. Even though he compared the measuring worm's eating of plants to the rainbow's appearance at the end of rains, he also attributed hope and renewal as rainbow symbols. Those symbols are almost universal for the meaning of a rainbow. Mallery must have had quite an imagination to come up with the measuring worm idea, but it's probably no less fanciful than the myths and legends of a pot of gold at a rainbow's ends.

The short duration of this morning's rainbow, a sight so fleeting it had to be viewed within a few minutes of time, would have been missed by anyone not yet up to greet the day. So awesome was my view of it that I feel a personal attachment as if it appeared and existed for me alone. And, in the scientific sense, it was my individual sighting because no two people can see exactly the same rainbow. Each person is looking from a slightly different angle even when they are standing next to each other. That means the light rays and water droplets creating the rainbow are just a little different for each observer.

Knowing that every rainbow I've ever seen belongs to me personally, I feel I can create my own myth of meaning. Mine doesn't include a measuring worm or a bridge across the sky, but it does see a rainbow as inspiration and a reminder never to take anything for granted. All of life is a gift, and sometimes the gift is fleeting as well as beautiful.

I would have missed this special event if my own negligence had not put me in the right place at the perfect moment. But my mistake became an opportunity. Some people believe there are no mistakes, only causes and effects. After my experience this morning of seeing a spectacular rainbow, I am convinced serendipity plays an important part in my life. If I can begin the day, my soul saturated with nature's brilliance revealed in a brush stroke of vivid color extending across the heavens, how can I not be filled with reverence and thankfulness?

This morning's experience raised my spirits and stamped upon my being an appreciation of the world in which I live. With its marvels spread like a celestial banner of hope and celebration, I cannot help but be overcome with the wonder of it all and grateful for every moment I can experience it.

Prickly pear cactus flowers

"I feel I can create my own myth of meaning. Mine doesn't include a measuring worm or a bridge across the sky, but it does see a rainbow as inspiration and a reminder never to take anything for granted."

Indian Blanket (*Gaillardia pulchella*)

"Look deep into nature and then you will understand everything better."

- Albert Einstein